THE POWER OF PRAYER, PRAISE, AND WORSHIP

DR CHARLENE HOLMES-PLUMP

Shrubs Publishing

ABSTRACT

The result of communicating with the Lord will become evident while decreasing the works of the flesh and igniting the fruit of the spirit. Men were born to befriend God, to worship, for closeness, and dual decision-making. Our Father, the Lord God longs to commune and answer prayers. Through the power of prayer, praise, and worship, learning is achievable in unfolding the secret dwellings of the Lord God's kingdom, thus maturing in Him. The power of prayer, praise, and worship can change circumstances…wait on the Lord.

DEDICATION

I dedicate this thesis to my mother, Pastor Ruthie M. Sanford. I salute you for your encouragement and the outstanding leadership qualities you passed on to me. Most of all, your friendship and remaining my lifelong prayer partner, through every storm and battle. You taught me to pray my way through every situation.

INTRODUCTION

There is a lack of expansion of the kingdom of God and the knowledge about God in the world because there seems to be less praying, praising, and worshiping. At best, most have grown too comfortable with the cares of this life, and so they fail to sense the critical need to pray for themselves and others. God loves for us to include Him in every part of our daily lives. Scripture says in Psalms 22:3, "that he inhabits the praises of his people." When the Holy Ghost ignites us with His power, we praise, pray, and worship more often and more effectively. There is a skillfulness, dexterity, or an architectural ability that prayer, praise, and worship prepares to set the atmosphere for change from life's plethora of problems. There is such a cloud of witnesses who can confirm that prayer, praise, and worship have and will change lives for the better.

Today, prayer seems to have become a difficult and trying subject – particularly in knowing how to pray or even having the confidence to pray. This book will show you how to take advantage of this privilege and understand the benefits of the power of prayer, praise, and worship.

For prayer to be effective, it must become a priority that is as necessary as the air we breathe, the water we drink, and the food we eat. Without these things, there's no life. Prayer should be a way of life. Not something that might fit into our schedules, but embedded

1

in your daily life. You should plan everything else around prayer, praise, and worship. The results are powerful in that something will happen because God will answer prayer with the peace that surpasses all understanding; read Philippians 4:7. The peace reference here is what God provides with His power that allows us to make it through difficult times. It is the power of wisdom given by God to obtain knowledge and His power of grace that helps us display Christ-like attributes in the midst of a sinful world.

We must engage our heart, mind, ears, eyes, and soul in God's presence. God has so much nurturing to provide for them that seek Him with diligence. When we pray and come into His presence with thanksgiving, our hearts enter into His courts with praise. This is important even when you're upset and in need of pampering. God wants to be the first to know all desires wants and needs. God, our Creator, loves the intimacy that prayer brings, drawing us closer to him. Prayer, praise, and worship are powerful because God is omnipotent and omnipresent.

There is a tactic that develops in communicating with the Lord that brings answers to prayers *in the now*. Prayer, praise, and worship trigger the whole process of spiritual warfare. God is commanding us to join together our swords in the spirit against the adversary. 2 Corinthians 10:4-5 says, "For the weapons of our warfare are not carnal but mighty in God for pulling down strongholds, casting down imaginations and every high thing that exalted itself against the knowledge of God and bringing into captivity every thought to the obedience of Christ." Our God has given us weaponry to counter-attack the influences of the devil. There are six weapons: five of the spiritual weaponry are used for offensive tactics and one for defensive spiritual warfare, against the wiles of the devil. However, to win, Christians must draw upon God's power.

> Finally, my brethren, be strong in the Lord, and
> in the power of his might. Put on the whole armor of God,
> that ye may be able to stand against the wiles of the devil. For
> we wrestle not against flesh and blood, but against principalities,
> against powers, against the rulers of the darkness of this
> world, against spiritual wickedness in high places. Wherefore
> take unto you the whole armor of God, that ye may be able to
> withstand in the evil day, and having done all, to stand. Stand
> Therefore, having your loins girt about with truth, and having
> on the breastplate of righteousness, And your feet shod with the
> preparation of the gospel of peace; above all, taking the shield
> of faith, wherewith ye shall be able to quench all the
> fiery darts of the wicked. And take the helmet of salvation,
> and the sword of the Spirit, which is the word of God: Praying
> always with all prayer and supplication in the Spirit,
> and watching thereunto with all perseverance and
> supplication for all saints. (Ephesians 6:10-24)

The apostle Paul tells us to be active in the Lord in God's mighty power. That power belongs to God and is not of man. Paul tells us that our enemy is conniving and a powerful ruler of this world. In other words, *the devil is real.*

The apostle Paul guides us on how to dress in God's power. He tells us to put on God's armor. He used the Greek term *panoplia*, which can mean to be armed entirely in the armor necessary for a soldier readying for battle. Many spiritual armies rage against humanity. Satan was not bluffing when he told Jesus, during His temptations (as told in Matthew 4:1), that he was able to give Him the kingdoms of this world.

Christians must identify spiritual wickedness. It affects us in areas such as political, economic, and social as well as the domains which are ruled and disbanded through the power of prayer, praise, and worship. Christ has already defeated them, but they refuse to accept their defeat. Upon God's return, they will be forced to give up their kingdoms in evil high places in this world completely. Until then, we must posture ourselves to standing firm in resistance to evil.

In the military, when soldiers are in position, they do not break rank on the battlefield. Fully-equipped soldiers on the battlefield remain impermeable to the enemy unless they freak out and run off the battlefield.

The belt of truth is what the soldier hangs his sword on. The belt also secures his tunic and armor, ensuring quick retrieval of the sword while in battle. Unlike the enemy who uses lying and deceitful tactics, the Christians' approach is sincere and true.

The breastplate of righteousness, which was a significant piece of armor for the Roman soldier, was made of leather and metal, protecting their vital organs. The *righteousness* mentions the status of Christian as they stand before God, emerging from the heart of man. The enemy tries to use our emotions to change us to his will. The soldiers' shields were soaked in water to quench the fiery darts. The darts used by the enemy were not used as much to kill as they were used to create chaos and fear, causing them to break ranks. They are known as the influences, enticements, trials, persecution, and sufferings that come outside of the church.

Next, there is the helmet of salvation. Now, the helmet is a natural covering for the soldier's head protecting him from all the most massive ax blows. The serpent's tactic in the garden of Eden with Eve was focused on getting her to fall from grace. He used persuasion of the mind. He wanted her to rethink or question what God had commanded. There is a must in guarding our thoughts by pressing into the Word of God with prayer, praise, and worship. The thoughts that Satan sends are false ideas – thoughts to dismantle our foothold with God. Salvation guarantees that the outcome of the battle is a known, certain defeat against the enemy. Our feet must be shod and prepared for peace, ready to help us keep our balance in warfare. When our feet are rooted and grounded in God and His peace, we are living in the understanding that continual attacks come from the adversary. Our footing should be ready for offensive and defensive battle in resistance from the devices of Satan using prayer and praise worship as tools of defense.

Another part of the armor of God to equip is with the sword of the Spirit. The task at hand for the Christians is to stand using the Word of God and not to attack with human strategies. Verse eighteen tells us to pray, which is not mentioned as armor, but the lack of prayer is detrimental to your protection. Praying should be used in conjunction with all six spiritual armors.

The Bible says the Word of God is the sword of the spirit. Praying in the Holy Ghost is praying in Jesus's name. It is He that helps us in our weakness in prayer, and it is His spirit that makes intercession to the will of God; read Roman 8:9. It is through the spirit of the Holy Ghost (His essence) that allows our conscience to become sensitive to sin and inspires us to pray prayers that He delights to hear. Praying in the spirit is what creates the conditions and atmosphere. The spirit should guide prayer. Praying in the spirit is very important because it is cognitively placing us under the guidance of the Holy Ghost. Like the apostle Paul does when praying, ask for courage, confidence, boldness, and fearlessness.

Fine-tuning life through prayer can unlock the doors of the secret place of the highest God. While still praying without ceasing, knowing that God inhabits the praises of his people and worshiping God in spirit and truth the results are surmountable, even when it does not seem possible. Knowing that God hears our prayers brings about praise on the inside manifesting a blessing on the outside – which is at the crux of the power of prayer, praise, and worship. Our hearts, our minds, souls, and strength are all united with our Lord while bowing before Him with thanksgiving. Believers confidently approach God in prayer because they realize His throne is of grace and mercy which are the benefits of Jesus as our High Priest sitting at the right hand of God. He is our mediator forever. The facts are in and have been confirmed, through a mass of witnesses from the scripture and present prayer warriors. When our hearts and our eyes are set on Jesus, it causes His true nature to reveal itself to us in spirit and truth. "Set your minds on things above, not on earthly things" (Col. 3:2 NIV).

The Holy Ghost guides the reasoning process in prayer, turning it into godly meditation. Jesus's light, perception, and revelation can come to pass. Those who are on the frontline are helping to advance Jesus's kingdom by preserving in pray, praise, and worship. Being on the front line means you're standing in an influential position to make changes in communicating with Jesus. Those who understand that, while we were yet sinners, Jesus Christ died for those who were striving to make it to the city called heaven.

Rest in the Lord and wait patiently for him; read Psalm 37:7. Prayer, praise, and worship continually, as it is intercessory, for healing, forgiveness, patience, and listening are paramount in the fulfillment of the prayers that seem delayed because God will answer prayers in His time.

POWERLESS PRAYER

When there is an absence of prayer, praise, and worship, it creates a deficiency. Where there's no prayer, there is no fear or need to know God, which is disobedience. There is a call to worship Him. When there is no understanding of God caused by powerless prayer it is because God has not been revealed. The culprit of powerless prayer indeed is sin. It is the blindness that the nature of sin brings. Symptoms are not knowing the need for repentance, forgiveness, or salvation. Paul said, "The god of this world has blinded the minds of those who believe not…" (2 Cor. 4:4). For the shame of sin has disappeared, and the need for repentance is void. As a result, we have a corrupt society with an inaccurate view of sin. Sin is such an ugly creature, and due to the sense of shame and pride that comes from sin, instead of repentance, the guilty try to hide their flaws from others.

Powerless prayer causes dullness and unawareness of the power of sin that allows Satan to hold captives in blindness from the truth. Powerless prayer happens when there is no understand or misapprehension of talking to God that brings His desires for His people into the now. Powerless prayer is the lack of a willingness to draw nigh to God by either not praying or not heeding the answer to a prayer.

In 1 Kings, there was a man of God who came from Judah, who prophesied and healed King Jeroboam of a paralyzed hand. King

Jeroboam after being healed offered the man of God to go home and dine with him as well as offered him a reward. However, the man of God replied *the Lord had forbidden me, that I should not go with you, nor can I eat, drink water at your house, and nor am I allowed even to go back the same direction I came.* So, the man of God left and did go in another direction. Meanwhile, there was an old prophet from Bethel whose sons told him all the work that God had done through the man of God to King Jeroboam. Consequently, the old prophet from Bethel asked of his sons, *which direction had the man of God gone?* For the sons had paid attention to which way he went. The old prophet told his sons to saddle his ass, and he went out to meet the man of God. When God gives us a command in prayer, we must obey His Word. As we grow as Christians and read the Bible, we learn how important it is to obey God rather than man. There are always consequences for disobedience.

The old prophet met up with the man of God who came from Judah. The man of God told the prophet that he was also a prophet and that an angel said to bring him back to his house to dine. However, that was a bald-faced lie. Therefore, the prophet did go with him to his house and ate bread and drank water. While they sat at the table, the word of the Lord came to the old prophet who then tricked him back.

The man cried out, "God said that you did not keep the instruction that the Lord thy God commanded. Instead, you returned and ate bread and drank water in this house." Not all food is for consumption because some are filled with corruption, vainness, perversion causing a breach in fellowship with God.

God replied to the man of God, "Since you choose to do what I told you *not to do* in this place, your corpse will not rest in the burial place of your fathers."

This is not an example of someone who prayed to seek an answer. In fact, the reason it is a powerless prayer is that the old prophet failed to pray *to God*. He did not consult God in all his ways, thereby recognizing God and seeking Him. He changed his mind and did what his fleshly self wanted to do. Without prayer, you will follow the voice of another. Like the man of God, most follow self.

After they had finished dining, the man who had brought him home saddled an ass for the old prophet. The old prophet went on his way and was greeted by a lion who slew him. His corpse lay on the side of the road. The donkey and the lion stood next to the corpse. The lion did not touch the donkey. The disobedient prophet had died just as God's prophecy foretold.

The penalty of powerless prayer is death; he did not obey the voice of God's reply.

In the book of Luke, Jesus presents a parable referencing two men, a Pharisee, and a publican, who both went to the temple to pray. The Pharisee was described as a religious leader. The Pharisees considered themselves the perfect example of righteous leaders of the Jews and the publicans were tax collectors. whose occupation was despised because tax collectors all worked for the Roman government. They were known to overcharge for taxes to procure great financial gain for themselves.

Now the Pharisee as he began to pray he started by saying he thanked God that he was not like the publican. That was not a true prayer of thanksgiving and praise to God. He started by throwing the publican under the bus. He felt his religious class was better (self-righteous). He pointed out specific areas that he thought were the most ungodly in society: extortionist, the unjust, and adulterers. He then pointed out areas where he was faithful to God.

God looks at the hearts of man, not by our acts. We are justified by faith not by works. The humble shall receive the kingdom of God. Also, God loves everyone – not just one particular group of people. The Pharisee's lifestyle had brought him into a state of self-righteousness. He was trying to substitute his moral actions for unearned favor. He felt he had no sins to admit. Sadly, he didn't even know he was reprobated.

The publican, on the other hand, stood far away and he wouldn't even look up to even gaze at the Pharisee because he thought he was unworthy. Little did he know that he was considered godlier than the religious leader. He also stood and beat his chest in the humiliation of how sinful he was and asked God's forgiveness for his deeds. He recognized he had nothing else to offer but humility and recognized his need for a Savior.

Jesus said that the publican is the one that went away justified in God's eyes. Where there is no humility in prayer it is powerless. It was true that the Pharisee wasn't an extortioner, unjust person, or adulterer. However, he didn't realize his need for God's saving grace.

The saddest thing that is present here is a high percentage of church attendees who are not born again. People attend church every Sunday but miss the most important concept – you must ask for forgiveness. Just as for the Pharisee that showed an outwardly pure life, it was no guarantee of salvation. The same principle applies to today's world. When we pray, we must confess our sins and receive Jesus as our personal Savior. If we maintain a self-righteous, prideful spirit in prayer, the result causes dryness and ignorance of sin. The result is prayers go unanswered. In other words, it is powerless prayer. Without confession, forgiveness our prayers will stay powerless.

PRAISE IN PRAYER

Praise sets the atmosphere for prayer and sometimes should be the only thing that we do while praying. Praise in prayer is not the only time, we should praise him, but it is one of the times we can because God has called us out of darkness into his marvelous light.

> "Let them praise the name of the Lord: for he commanded, and they were created" (Ps. 148:5).

The Lord is worthy of such honor as the Creator of all things. Whom to praise in prayer? His name. The answer to the question from the phrase, "the name of the Lord" in the above scripture. His name stands for His character and His traits. We should recognize God's excellence, works, and assistance. Praise is a command, not an option. He commanded all things into existence with his breath; read Psalm 33:4. Praise ends with God because the act of consecration confessed by acknowledgment and admiration of his many characteristics shown through praise. We should exalt His name. Praying and praising are to God for all the wonderful things He has done and his loving-kindness. Worshiping God while praying and praising, for all his goodness, unlocks a deeper relationship with him. Praise changes the focus from life complications to the uniqueness of God in knowing he is omnipotence, omnipresence, and omniscience. Spiritually it is profitable to give praise to God because it aligns us with God. Luke 1:39-56 is an excellent example of praising God in prayer; Mary, the

14

mother of Jesus, gives her prayer of praise which is called the *Magnificat*. Mary began exalting the Lord and rejoicing in the Savior. It was with *all her being* that she praised God. By referring to him as her Savior, meant that she confessed she was in need of salvation. Mary must not be elevated to be worship as some have done. Because she recognized her sinful condition, that opened the door for God to use her in such a significant way. Mary was awe struck by what God was doing. She was trying to process all that God had done in such a little time, she could do nothing other than praise him in so doing magnify (raise the roof) her Savior. Mary knew it was all good and all God and she could take no credit. God could have chosen another who was rich, powerful but rather he chooses an average young girl. Like Mary, our praise in prayer should focus on the one who is faithful and merciful. Mary knew that God should get all the glory and honor. Mary humbled herself before the almighty God to worship Him in spirit and truth. All her attention was focus on the Lord, her Savior, and not herself. It wasn't something she could keep to herself. Her prayer of praise was like Hannah; both godly women recognized their omnipotent God through prayer praise and worship. We must consider our petitions answered and praise God in Faith. She was reminiscent of the word rejoicing in reference to the angels who came and announced she would carry the Messiah. She knew this maiden had gone from insignificance to somebody that the world forever would speak

15

about. God has given us many promises, but their fulfillment requires faith. God is the God of great things. We must submit ourselves to the God of our salvation in praise in prayer.

In Acts 16, Luke explains a story that also has key elements of prayer, praise, and worship. It happened to Paul and Silas, their wrongful arrest for casting a spirit of divination out of a girl. The local Philippian authorities whipped them and then threw them into a jail cell. "At midnight Paul and Silas prayed and sang praises to God while the prisoner listened" (Acts 16:25).

Their bodies were still bleeding and attached in the stocks, which clamped their arms and legs, leaving them unable to move. An assumption that no one cared to their open wounds, all of this probably prevented them from sleeping. Their spirits, under "the expulsive power of the Holy Ghost, provides a new care," hearts rose above suffering, and made the prison cries echo with their song. "In these midnight hymns, by God's design has always been to lead us to a deeper understanding that in His timing the result in life is a greater reward on earth; an eternity of rewards in the kingdom to come. God is calling with urgency for men to kneel, yielding to prayer, praise, and worship.

All scripture is given by inspiration of God and is profitable for doctrine, for reproof, for correction and instruction in righteousness: 17. That the man of God may be perfect, thoroughly furnished unto all good works. (2 Timothy 3:16-17.)

God provides the scripture to promote righteousness and to motivate us to control carnal natures to His will. He will increase wisdom and knowledge without reservation. God measures not according to status but according to his grace, mercies, and His kindness toward us; read James 1:5.

Despite their throbbing pain in their bodies from the beatings they received, at midnight Paul and Silas were heard praying and singing praises to God! Worshiping the Lord in the spirit and truth. Read John 4:24. Listen, hear them crying out:

> "If it had not been the LORD who was on our side when men rose up against us:[3] Then they had swallowed us up quick when their wrath was kindled against us:..[8] Our help is in the name of the LORD, who made heaven and earth. (Psalm124:2-3,8)

God has, again and again, demonstrated that He is on our side to help when the wicked comes to eat up our flesh. He causes them to blunder and fall. Paul and Silas were confident that God would help. The understanding that the current trials faced is just a drop in the bucket to what God's reward in heaven; read Romans 8:18. Talking to God always reveals He is right by for every situation.

Just imagine hearing praises, instead of cursing, this must have overwhelmed the other prisoners. The other jailer felt the peace that didn't make sense, but yet it was soothing. Then suddenly it happened the result of prayer. There was an earthquake that shook the foundation of the cells, and all the jail cell doors flung open. Paul and Silas and the other prisoner were released. Prayer increases faith because we ask God in faith, he grants our petitions according to his will. This text showed results of prayer, praise in worship is at the heart of the Redeemer. God hears the voice of man when we talk to him.

WORSHIP IN PRAYER

According to Psalms ~ Book of Praises, Tabernacle Bible Institute, *worship* is defined as the act of paying honor to a deity; giving reverence and homage to God, bowing down before God, and spoken worship rendered to God. We must bow down to the King of kings and Lord of lords in prayer, praise, and worship. "Oh come, let us worship and bow down; let us kneel before the Lord, our maker" (Ps. 95:6).

The Hebrew word for worship is *shachah* means to cause oneself to lie prostrate, to kneel, and to bow down. Body language in this position of devotion assures Him of our submission to the Lord with every command. Second Peter, chapter 2 verse 9 says, "Ye should shew forth the praises of him who hath called you out of darkness into his marvelous light." We were born to worship God, declaring that God is worth more than everything else. Worship must be in the heart not in a physical place or building of worship. The fact that we exist, our capability to think, the even capacity to worship in the first place comes from Him.

Many chapters are written in Psalms in the form of prayer, or praise, and worship. They are words spoken to God. He is the listener; the people are the worshipers. Worship encompasses the heart, soul, mind, and strength. While praying, we should worship in honor of God. Praise is knowing what he is in our lives and showing it with action. Prayer is a way of speaking with God and making our requests known, worship is a humbling of self, giving God the glory for what He has done. There are many approaches to worship such as:

> Praise ye the Lord. Praise God in his sanctuary: Praise God in his sanctuary, Praise him in the firmament of his power. Praise him for his mighty acts; praise him according to his excellent greatness" (Psalms 150:1-3)

God deserves praise, and He desires our praise and worship. All three consist of a basic formula to form a relationship with the Lord. It is significant to understand the concept, learning how to pray, praise, and worship. There is no right or wrong way to pray. We cannot allow immaturity to stop us from joining God. Take the time and build a relationship with God through prayer, praise, and worship.

People like the results of prayer, but don't come to Jesus to know Him. They do not even understand what the power of prayer, praise, and worship can do. The story of Hannah in 1 Samuel, chapters 1 and 2 gives a good illustration of how the power of prayer, praise, and worship gets results. Also, this story is about how the power of prayer, praise, and worship can produce a breakthrough, new life, deliverance, and give victory.

Elkanah the Ephraimite had two wives named Peninnah and Hannah. The story reads, in 1 Samuel, that Peninnah had children, but Hannah was barren. Every year the men of Israel left their cities, according to God's law (read Exodus 34:23), and attended three annual festivals in Jerusalem (Shiloh).

At this time, to be childless was considered a disgrace for a woman. A barren woman felt humiliated. Hannah asked God why had He closed her womb? Sure, others assumed the same stinking thinking. Hannah suffered from the label – barren. She had to watch Peninnah with her many children parade around her daily. The scripture says that Peninnah taunted her, enjoying that Hannah could not have children. However, that was not the only reason she mocked Hannah. It was that Elkanah loved Hannah more than he loved Peninnah. Elkanah told Hannah he loved her more than having ten children. Both women had a dilemma.

Hannah chooses to walk by the spirit and not be persuaded by the flesh. To walk by the Spirit indicates that we are maintaining a constant relationship with God. We are training those spiritual disciplines to keep our focus on the Lord. Walking by the Spirit encompasses patterning Christ's life attributes. "For the flesh lusteth against the Spirit, and the Spirit against the flesh: and these are contrary the one to the other: so, that ye cannot do the things that ye would" (Gal. 5:17).

To animate in the flesh is to live by man's capability, his humanness. However, when living by the Spirit, you are dependent on the assets and the abilities of God's grace through faith, receiving unlimited results.

Hannah's misery caused her to weep and she would not eat. Elkanah gave her a double portion because of her sad heart concerning her inability to conceive. This problem seemed to escalate even more during the time of the annual sacrifice. That is how the devil works. When it is time to praise and worship, he always wants to turn things around to sorrow. Besides, God forbids. Shiloh was the place God commanded his people to worship, a time of feasting and celebration for how the Lord had brought them out of bondage. It was not the time for sorrow, fighting, or rivalry.

It was not a requirement for the men to bring their families to the festival, but some did. The festival was a time of prayer, praise, and worship, which involved the sacrifice of animals, a banquet of meat and wine. Eli was Israel's High priest and judge throughout this time. He came from the family of Ithamar, Aaron's fourth son; read 1 King 2:27.

Hannah displayed her devotion to the Lord by making the trip to Shiloh to worship. It was at this time that Peninnah's taunting vexation set in. She cried and lost her appetite. She did not eat. After trying to finishing up the meal, the scripture says that Hannah stood up. Hannah had a hallelujah anyway. The Spirit came forth from her bosom; enough was enough. You see, sometimes when problems weigh upon us, it seems a breakthrough will come, trials on the left and right. There is a position that gets results. She knew the God of breakthroughs. Hannah made her way to the tabernacle to pray with tears still in her eyes.

I can see Jesus in my spiritual mind saying, *My child, what's the matter now?* Instead of remaining hopeless, Hannah took a stand. She knelt down and prayed. Hannah made her petition known to God; with many tears, she poured out from the depth of her soul. In those times, the Holy Ghost was not present as now, but we are cognizant from reading the scripture that it came upon a few at certain times. Such as, when the Prophet Samuel took oil and anointed David to be king as David's brothers witnessed. He kept God's presence from that day forward. Through the blood of Jesus, each one of us can experience the Holy Ghost and his power in our lives, right now. Romans 8:26 says, "Likewise, the Spirit also helpeth our infirmities: for we know not what we should pray for as we ought: but the Spirit itself maketh intercession for us with groanings which cannot be uttered."

God searches the heart and knows the mind of our spirit because the Spirit intercedes for the saints according to God's will. The Spirit steps in through the groans, tears, pain, and despair when we do not know how to answer.

While Hannah prayed at the Tabernacle Eli, the priest was sitting at the entrance where people would come in for judgment. Hannah at the altar began to pour out from the depth of her soul making her request known to God. Read about it in Philippians 4:6. Hannah started to make a vow to the Lord. Desperate means call for desperate measures. Hannah wanted a son so badly. She said, *just let me carry him in my womb, I will give him back to you.*

The words *no razor shall come upon his head* reference the Nazirite law; read Numbers 6:2-6. Hannah devoted her son to God as a Nazirite for his entire life. This vow is usually made for a set time, not for life (see glossary for more explanation). The priest Eli was watching Hannah from a distance but couldn't understand what she was saying. He thought she was drunk because she'd spent so much time in prayer. Hannah's mouth was moving, but nothing was coming out. This is an example that prayer does not have to be charismatic or flamboyant for God to hear and answer. God is not deaf. "This poor man cried, and the LORD heard him and saved him out of all his troubles" (Ps. 34:6).

Also, it is a shame to say that even then it was not normal for someone to pray in church for long periods. Eli misunderstood her, and he likely thought she might have been one of the drunken women at the door of the tabernacle because his sons slept with some of them.

Hannah was not drunk but was, in fact, demonstrating fervent praying. She was spending time talking (praying) to the Lord, telling him all about her problem, and making a vow. There is no way while praying one can maintain a consistent level of shouting the entire time. Eventually, fatigue would set-in, and one would regress to a low whisper, instead. Eli should have been a little bit more observant, for somebody drunk would probably cause a scene than being silent. Eli needed to intercede on God's behalf but instead came to the wrong conclusion. How many times has someone needed prayer but instead, their name was slandered? Hannah did not have a comeback line that insulted the high priest. Instead, Hannah answered Eli and said, "No, my lord, I am a woman of sorrowful spirit. I have drunk neither wine nor intoxicating drink, but have poured out my soul before the Lord" (1 Sam. 1:15).

Hannah responded to Eli by saying that she was a woman who had a sad heart and had not drunk with wine or any strong intoxicating drinks. Nevertheless, here in prayer, she poured out her soul (fervent praying) to God. When it is "Me oh, Lord" standing in needy prayer, speaking to the highest God, nothing matters even when insulted, you remain humble. She exclaimed *I am not a wicked woman*. She wanted him to know that she was not the daughter of Satan. Eli recognized that she was not a daughter of the devil by answering, *You are released from the burden, go in peace*, and then "God of Israel grant your petition which you have asked of Him" (1

Sam. 1:17). Since Eli was the chief priest, he had the authority to speak on behalf of God granting grace. Hannah walked away with a new attitude. She looked different – her face shone; no longer was her demeanor downcast. She had the peace of God that surpasses all understanding; read Philippians 4:7. God gave Hannah victory over her circumstances; read Romans 8:37. Also, Hannah's appetite returned. She went away and ate as she waited for her prayers answered. She got over her misery and realized that only God could give her the desires of her heart. Hannah made a vow to God that she would give her child to the Lord for the rest of his life.

Seriously, it is better not to make a vow than to make a vow, then break it. "When thou shalt vow a vow to the LORD thy God, thou shalt not slack to pay it: for the LORD thy God will surely require it of thee; and it would be sin in thee" (Deut. 23:21).

The next day they got up early to bow down before the Lord in worship and then returned home to Ramah. Then Elkanah slept with Hannah and "the Lord remembered Hannah" (1 Sam. 1:19). The atmosphere just shifted in her stead. God started to change things for Hannah by answering her prayer. In God's timing, Hannah conceived and gave birth to a son who was named Samuel. His name means "name of God."

It was that time of the year again where Elkanah and all his house went to offer the yearly sacrifice in Jerusalem. Hannah did not go and told Elkanah that she would not go until Samuel was weaned.

Elkanah told Hannah to do as she wished, meaning he gave his blessing. He could have in turn thought she has made a foolish vow and could have reprimanded her for giving their son to God for life, according to the Law of Moses (see glossary for detail). Finally, Hannah weaned Samuel and had to offer a sacrifice for what God had achieved on her behalf. After choosing three bulls to sacrifice as was the custom; read Numbers 15:9-10. She began to tell others by exalting and praising God for his loving-kindness that He had shown by giving her a son. She brought the child to Eli to commemorate her vow to God and to show her obedience to God.

In chapter two, Hannah goes into a prayer filled with praise and worship for what the LORD had done. Every year Hannah would come to Shiloh to see her son Samuel and to pray, praise, and worship God. Eli blessed Elkanah and Hannah and prayed she would have more children; the Lord was merciful to Hannah. She gave birth to three sons and two daughters. That is the power of true praise, prayer, and worship.

While praying, praising, and worshiping, we also should forgive others and confess our sins before God continuously. We were born in sin and shaped with wickedness; read Psalms 51:5 and "who shall deliver me from the body of death" (Rom. 7:14). According to Ephesians 1:7, "In Him we have redemption through his blood, the forgiveness of transgressions, bestowing the riches of his grace." However, the word used for sin, (transgression) has a deeper meaning; it expresses the effects of sin. Transgression means being separated from God.

Jesus, as a voluntary representative of humanity, purchased us with His blood. We now can be forgiven and are debt-free from God's wrath and the penalties of sin. At the prearranged time God commissioned Jesus to go to earth, ultimately to die for all the world oppressed by sin.

The carnal mind is an enemy of God and not subject to the law of God. Through the law was the knowledge of sin revealed. However, through the blood of Jesus, sin no longer has dominion, for through Him by faith, grace abides.

According to the book, *The Message of Romans* by David K. Bernard, a man in himself is incapable of combating sin because of the constant struggle between thoughts and the members of the body. When trying to do good – lying, cheating, hatred, fornication, drugs, and backbiting – all evils are there holding the mind in captivity. A person who is bound by evil is under the power of sin and is not free; read Romans 7:23.

Men still need redemption. Redemption represents the passageway through which salvation is accomplished, through the payment of a ransom. The price paid for our salvation was the death of Jesus Christ. Through Christ's redemption, all who have faith in Him receive the "adoptions of sons." Those who have been born into the family of God are now heirs, having now reached the age of maturity. They no longer are under guardianship but can now receive Abraham's promised inheritance –which is salvation! We must have faith and believe that the weight of sin no longer binds us. We are to confess our sins one to another and to intercede with prayer to God on their behalf. "Confess your faults one to another, and pray one for another, that ye may be healed. The effectual fervent prayer of a righteous man availeth much" (James 5:16).

A compassionate prayer can do everything. It can penetrate an iron fence; it can scale the tallest building. That's amazing; prayer is not powerless. The prophet Elijah demonstrated the effectiveness of power-filled prayers. He prayed powerfully and intensely for a drought, and it did not rain for three years and six months. It did not rain again until he prayed, once again. God heard and answered Elijah's prayer. Pray for each other, for some need physical healing and others spiritual. "And when he had said this, he breathed on them, and saith unto them, receive ye the Holy Ghost: Whosoever sins ye remit, they are remitted unto them; and whosever sins ye retain, they are retained" (John 20:22-23).

God has given the righteous the power to remit or retain on earth as it is in heaven through the gift of the Holy Ghost. Acknowledging that sin exists in us is the first step to spiritual restoration. Jesus commissioned the disciples to carry out His work through the power of the Holy Ghost. Jesus said they had the responsibilities for kingdom building. Not the power to forgive sins, but aiding those who were lost to find safety in Jesus Christ the Lord.

Jesus gave the atonement for us on the cross; read 1 John 1:7. His blood keeps on purging our sin, not the act of confessions. Jesus became a self-inflicted wound to set us right with God. Confession is part of the process of redemption. Our portion is to simply admit our role in what led Jesus to the cross. There could be no forgiveness of sins without the shedding of the blood of Christ; read Hebrews 9:22.

The songwriter, Robert Lowry wrote, "What can wash away my sin? Nothing but the blood of Jesus." God's Son came to save lost souls; read Matthew 18:11. Without Christ, the Savior, all are lost. All are sinners in need of God's forgiveness. To confess is to agree that we have done wrong and are in need of His mercy; read 1 John 1:9. If we confess, God is faithful and unbiased to exonerate us from all unrighteousness. When we pray and confess, it contradicts human nature because flesh contemplates it is all right, awesome, and better than the next person. God will set us on a new path if we ask forgiveness. That should be a part of our praying, praising, and worshiping.

In Psalm 32:5, this passage says that before King David confessed his sin, he became exhausted. Why? Sinful living will drain the life out of a saint or sinner. Weaken sin, before it deteriorates spiritual strength. When sin starts forming in our life we must be proactive in saying; with authority in the name of Jesus flee. Confession is a method to activate the Grace of God. It is also a part of sanctification in that it allows God to heal us from the effects of sin to go from powerless to powerful in prayer. Confessing our sins is practicing humility to God. It requires a humble person to admit their mistakes. God is turned away by a stubborn spirit; he looks for low in spirit and gives grace; read James 4:6. God sent Jonah to a foreign nation with a message that God was going to destroy them. The scripture says that the people of Nineveh did three things they believed God, proclaimed a fast. and put on sackcloth (humility). By this action, the Ninevites showed an outer indication of their changed hearts. God is looking for such people. Through this turn, God changed his judgment because they demonstrated true repentance. God gives grace to the meek.

God is granting his favor again, again to the one who depresses his conduct to accepting God's will. God is looking for true worshippers that are willing to confess and be real with God in prayer, praise and worship receiving, power. Ultimately, it is a must that we seek forgiveness for our sins in prayer. Blessed and beloved those that the Lord forgives and pardon every transgression of man. He who knew no sin is worthy to be called King of kings and Lord of Lords.

"Blessed is he whose transgression is forgiven, whose sin is covered. 2. Blessed is the man unto

whom the Lord imputeth not iniquity, and in
whose spirit there is no guile." (Psalms 32:1-2).

Those who confess their sins to God will obtain God's unmerited favor. Forgiveness and confession must be institutional as part of prayer, praise, and worship.

WORSHIP IN PRAYER

PETITION

One of the most powerful prayers mentions in the Bible of God can be found in one of the Psalms of David. In Psalms 56, reference when the Philistines took him to Gath one of the Philistine cities, David's petition begins with him asking God twice to be merciful, and then he speaks about how men could swallow him up, attempting to make his end. During one of King Saul's fits of anger and threats against his life; the record reads, "And David arose, and fled that day for fear of Saul, and went to Achish the king of Gath" (1 Sam. 21:10). Although he had fled before, both from his house and from Naioth, he now left his country completely and went, of all places, to the Philistine city of Gath, the former home of Goliath; read 1 Samuel 17:4. In 1 Samuel, chapter 21, David did not ask God for direction, his own mind was guiding and persuading him. David thought if he would run to the enemy of his adversary, he thought they would befriend him. Although apparently well received by the king, the king's servants took a more negative view. "Jealousy is cruel to the grave; the coals thereof are coals of fire, which hath a most vehement flame" (Song of Sol. 8:6).

The servants of Achish "said unto him, is not this David, the king of the land." Did they not sing one to another of him in dances, saying, Saul hath slain his thousands, and David his ten thousand?

Moreover, David placed these words in his heart, and was uncomfortable, terrified of Achish, the king of Gath" (1 Sam. 21:11-12). Somewhere either in the palace or front of the King Achish that David was apprehended.

David took two actions in response. First, he pretended madness by fumbling, or scratching, on the gates of the city and drooling saliva into his beard. His trick was successful in creating both abhorrence and compassion; Achish expelled him from the city. Second, he continued running until he got to a safer location, to the cave of Adullam, not far from his hometown of Bethlehem. There is a need to petition God against the enemy of souls, the adversary the devil. The reason David asks for mercy is he was searching in himself to see if any wickedness be in his heart. When we say to God be merciful, we are asking God to forgive us our trespasses. The more violent attack of Satan the stronger our petition should be to God, while praying, praising, and worshiping. There is no night or day in which we can retire from the world, and think where isolated and safe in our homes, and say, evil cannot enter at this time.

We need to watch as well as always pray to escape the snares of the devil; read Luke 21:36. Also, stay alert or on guard about those things about ourselves that will disqualify us from entering God's kingdom. God encourages us to make bold use of this tool for our every need. "Let us, therefore, come boldly unto the throne of grace, that we may obtain mercy, and find grace to help in time of need" (Heb. 4:16).

Prayer is the tool that God provides that helps us to be in constant exchange with Him; so that we can truly bring every thought into captivity, under the obedience of God's will. The scripture in 1 Samuel does not mention when David starts to recognize a need for change, but Psalms 56 records David's steps of recovery from lost to found.

David's sin had him running scared in all directions. However, in the Psalms, David's prayer was a petition for help. He knew running was not solving his problem. In verse ten, David's prayer turns into a praise and worship session, while embracing faith. David realizes not to fear man because man's flesh is nothing but dirt; read 1 Peter 1:24. The flesh is a vain temporary nature; that all its glory will fade away and soon be gone. It was God's breath that formed man in his image.

> "As for man, his days are as grass: as a flower of the
> field, so he flourisheth. For the wind passeth over it,
> and it is gone; and the   place thereof shall know
> it no more" (Ps. 103:15-16).

David petitions the Lord and tells Him that his enemy's thoughts toward him were evil. We know that Satan is the great accuser against God's kingdom day and night; read Revelations 12:10.

We read in 1 Samuel 21:6, that King Achish's men were evil cowards that were plotting and scheming against David in secret.

These wicked men would only find satisfaction by David's death. God visits man and holds their tears in a bottle for remembrance, "Put thou my tears in thy bottle" (vs. 9). When we pray those same tears, fly to heaven because God hears the faintest cries. He is such an awesome God! Near the end of Psalms, 56 David's transformation begins and he sees God's will. If we acknowledge our sins before the Lord, He is righteous and faithful to forgive; read 1 John 1:9. David realized that God allowed his deliverance from King Saul and his escape from Gath. He started to walk before "God in the light of life," David sees the light.

During prayer, praise, and worship, we are allowed to talk and hear God's answer; God inhabits the praises of His people. It is wonderful; and very comforting to know that we can speak with Him boldly with no pretense, in all honesty, without retribution or fear of anything. At any time, in any way, in all trials and emotional distress. Yes, God loves us! When we petition Jesus, He will hear the meek, the weak might, the strong, and the lost. Petitions must be seasoned with faith. God's capability is more than, we can ask or think.

KINGDOM PRAYING

Kingdom praying is placing the needs of the kingdom of God first. Jesus makes it clear that the kingdom of God has two stages, one now and one to come. The kingdom now is the presence of God in conjunction with earthly kingdoms. Jesus one day will rule over all, and share that with his people. Suddenly, Jesus will return when no one is paying any attention. Most people will be going about their daily business, unaware of the time is nigh; read Luke 17: 21-22. When he returns, the world will be perverted and wicked just as the days before the flood came, the days of Jonah. The kingdom of God within means that it is within our presence through the Holy Ghost. Kingdom praying is not based on the needs of man but centered around God's plans and to desire to rule morally on earth. "But seek ye first the kingdom of God and his righteousness, and all these things shall be added unto you" (Matt. 6:33).

Kingdom Prayer is the spirit-filled empowered cry of God's saints looking for God's glory by requesting Him for the nations, their promised inheritance, and craving God's righteousness ruling the earth. The reason for the importance of kingdom praying is in Matthew. "And from the days of John the Baptist until now the kingdom of heaven suffereth violence and the violent take it by force" (Matt. 11:12). This means that vicious individuals forcibly opposed the kingdom with their hostility toward the truth. Christ's kingdom is advancing daily, and so are the attacks of Satan. We must pray for Christ's kingdom to come and ask God to bind the devil's kingdom of this world.

> "For the kingdom of God is not meat and drink;
> but righteousness, and peace and joy in the
> Holy Ghost" (Rom. 14:7).

We need to understand our place with God. Why our God and why were His children and what responsibilities were given to us. Striving with all our might living to please Him, not to serve ourselves, but on the contrary to serve Him and the church. kingdom praying allows us to go deeper than physical needs such as food and drink but instead, seek spiritual realities like righteousness in action and thought, the peace that seeks harmony and joy that comes from the Holy Ghost. The Spirit of God will give us the knowledge of why we need to lay aside selfish desires and seek God's kingdom purpose. We should pray for Israel because they are the chosen nation because they shall prosper, which shows love toward them; read Psalms 122:6. Kingdom prayers should be made for our enemies because God provides for all even when we do not deserve it; read Matthew 5:44. Sometimes our blessing might come from our enemies, so we need to keep them in prayer. Kingdom-focused prayer is the Spirit-enabled cry of God's adopted children seeking their Father's glory by persistently asking Him for the nations, their promised inheritance.

PERSEVERANCE IN PRAYER

One of the most perplexing facets of prayer is a determination in prayer when it seems that God is not listening, nor answering. Even though most know and have prayed the Lord's prayer, "Hallowed be thou name thine kingdom come thine will be done…" However, the problematic issue for us is in waiting for God's completeness of a matter. Jesus tells a parable to the disciples saying, "to this end that men ought always to pray, and not to faint" (Luke 18:1-8). Jesus tells his disciples to pray and not give up but expect His response. The story also talks about a woman who persistently comes to an unjust judge several times. The judge tells the woman "No" several times to her request, however; she does not take "no" for an answer. Instead, every time court of law assembled, the woman came declaring and decreeing that justice would be served to her today. She keeps bringing her petition daily to the unjust judge though rejections came every day. She keeps expecting a miracle every time court was in session that today was her day. The scripture says that the judge started talking to himself saying, "Though I fear not, God nor regard man; yet because this widow troubleth I will avenge her, lest she wears me out by her continual coming" (Luke 18:4-5).

Keep on seeking God in prayer just like the widow, God will step in. Should we bring the same old prayer to God? The answer is yes; positively yes, keep carrying the same prayer before the Lord until a response is provided. In the parable of the persistent widow, an underprivileged, powerless person (the widow) persists in irritating a corrupt, powerful man (the judge) to do justice for her.

In the Old Testament laws, God commanded the Israelites not to take advantage of widows and orphans. In Psalm 68:5, God defines Himself as the Father of the fatherless, and Guardian of the widow. Jesus focuses the parable not on the position of power and leadership because as a leader there is an obligation to work justly, especially on behalf of the orphan and children. Jesus comes from the point of view, which says "to pray always and do not lose heart" (Luke 18:1). Instead, of pointing fingers, there is something each one can do about all situations that may plague our lives. Lifting up our voices to a Sovereign God, by coming to the throne of grace in prayer. All can come without cost to pray, and receive a return on that investment through Jesus, everlasting life. If by being persistent, we can be triumphant with crooked human-restricted power, how much more would it result with a righteous God with immeasurable power?

In the book of Luke chapter 2, the story scene is set, after the time of the rites of Mary purification according to the Law of Moses to present Jesus to the priest. They were met in the temple courts by

Simeon a devout righteous man from Jerusalem, who was told by the Holy Ghost that he would not die until he had seen the child, Jesus. Simeon was to receive spiritual insight impartation from God, but for this to occur, he had to have a faithful prayer, praise and worship relationship with God. Simeon was persevering and waiting for this imparted insight to come forth which was to see the Messiah. Because of his obedience to God, he was able to be led by the Holy Ghost and be at the right place at the right time to see the anointed one who was born to die for our sins. There was also a prophetess by the name of Anna from the tribe of Asher another faithful prayer, praise, and worshiper. She became a widow after only being married for seven years. She remained a widow to the age of eighty-four. Anna was committed to the Lord unto death. The scripture says she on no occasion left the church, but dedicated herself to worship night and day to fasting and in prayer. This woman also had the miraculious opportunity to see God in the flesh before her death. She too persevered in prayer before the Lord and the scripture does not say what she prayed for, but that she prayed.

> Cast not away, therefore, your confidence, which hath.
> Great confidence, which hath great recompense of
> reward. For ye have need of patience, that,after ye
> have done the will of God, ye might receive the
> promise. For yet a little while, and He that
> shall come will come, and will not tarry.
> (Hebrews 10:35-37)

Continually, confidently stay in prayer against all trials, knowing that God is a reward to them that persistently seek him. God's will shall prevail even in an unjust world. Not persevering in faith and prayer, gives the accuser (Satan) an opportunity to slander more. He is always day and night looking for an open occasion to devour. If faith channels are not resting in God's will, Satan sees the moment to consider to infiltrate the minds of many.

> "For I know the thoughts that I think toward you,
> saith the LORD, thoughts of peace, and not of evil,
> to give you an expected end" (Jer. 29:11).

The judgment God has for us is not wicked but of peace to bring us to victory in Him. Jesus paid the price on Calvary to bring us to an armistice with God. Jesus considers those who do not endure as salt that is tasteless, good only for being trodden upon by men; read Matthew 5:13.

Our job is to always work toward that hope knowing that prayer changes things. Our role has never been to fix every wrong in this world in the present or future. However, do not give up hope in the midst of imperfect systems where legislators cheat to win office. Only God brings salvation. Take notes from the pregnant women who sometimes when travailing must walk in order to move the baby down through the birth canal, even though it may be uncomfortable and times might hurt. That is why it is a must to pray, praise, and worship God and not lose heart in our work for Christ. God is a present help in the time of trouble. "As a pregnant woman about to give birth writhes and cries out in her pain, so were we in your presence, LORD. We were with child, we writhed in labor, but we gave birth to wind. We have not brought salvation to the earth, and the people of the world have not come to life" (Isa. 26:17).

However, like the woman in labor waiting for her time to come to give birth which still requires patience because the baby is not coming until God says so. Before labor pangs intensify everything matters, those pregnant want only certain people in the room. They are focused on everyday life. But once the pangs intensify things change, you no longer care, about whose there, nor how one looks. Now beginning to focus on one objective; the arrival of the baby. There is only one hope, one prayer, and one praise. Digging in and persevering to the end to see that baby. Paul tells us in 1 Corinthians 9, that he too is in a race, competing for a prize reaching for the gold. Paul was trying to receive the award, internal life in God through Christ Jesus. To do this, he had sacrificed all: his reputation as a Pharisee, his care, and safety.

All must willingly and gladly lay down every weight, hindrance, distraction that will inhibit us from reaching a spiritual and eternal goal to hear our Savior say, "Well done. Enduring in Christ is essential, steady watching out for all things that could retain us from pursuing God passionately. To stay in the race, one must travel light and keep pressing inward to the finish line. It is so easy to get caught up in the cares of this life not just on physical things, but also distractions like reputation, carnal and religious achievement. "And profited in the Jews' religion above many my equals in mine own nation, being more exceedingly zealous of the traditions of my fathers" (Gal. 1:14).

Paul was a Pharisee like his father, and when it came to knowing and understanding God's law, he had succeeded his contemporaries having been taught by one of the most excellent doctors of the law, the law of his time Gamaliel. In retrospect, the apostle Paul realized the best part of life was not about any of those things that made him look great on a resume because those were the things that enabled him to persecute the church in which no longer impressive him. He realizes the best day of his life was on that road to Damascus when he saw Jesus. Paul sums it all up by saying, "Not as though I had already attained" (Phil. 3:12). Paul was content with knowing Jesus Christ as his Savior, but he was not comfortable with his Christian life. Paul not being satisfied, caused him to persevere and push ahead to God's will.

Peter calls our attention to the brutality of the enemy by telling us, "Be sober, be vigilant; because your adversary, the devil, as a roaring lion, walketh about, seeking whom he may devour; Whom resist steadfast in the faith, knowing that the same afflictions are accomplished in your brethren that are in the world" (1 Pet. 5:8-9).

Satan is out lurking seeking because he knows he has a short time to gather all sinners. Those that fell to repent, seeking their own way in this life. Resist because others are going through storms as well.

In this life all will face stormy weather, some are in the storm, others coming out or some are heading into a storm, but all will encounter the same circumstance at some point in their life. Help from the Lord can supply the power to plow through all obstacles. Individually persevering in pray, praise and worship knowing that help is on its way in God's timing. It is through perseverance that helps transitions us. It assists us in understanding not to live by our emotions and eyesight but to see beyond the veil to the next station. It is these components that can't be taught by mere knowledge or passed on by mentors. Each one must experience God's plans for their lives independently and perseverance provides the testimony of hope as an overcomer. God will give us the spiritual power and resources to overcome any complication to obtain an incorruptible crown. Asking Him in prayer to empower us to let nothing come between Him and us and to assist us in the journey.

HOW DOES GOD REVEAL HIMSELF AFTER PRAYER?

The kingdom of God is not an item of dialogue but power. All this talk about talking to God, but more importantly it's to understand how God speaks. God does respond to prayer, but sometimes it is missed because he does not always answer according to our expectations. When listening and paying attention, God provides ways with the direction (answers) from the Holy Ghost. Listening is not just listening but in fact, God providing anthropomorphic expression to us after prayer. How does God respond after we pray? There are many ways God uses anthropomorphism to reveal himself such as audible voice, an inner still voice, handwriting on the wall, mist, theophany's, drops of water, dreams, visions, and prophets prophesying. There are many ways God reveals Himself when answering prayers as previously mentioned and some not referenced. From the list, we will discuss only the audible voice, inner still small voice, and dreams as seen from the word of God.

In the book of Exodus, chapter 19, there's an excellent description of an event that depicts the voice of God. The ninth verse says that God told Moses that "I AM" was going to come in a dense cloud so that the public would hear Him speaking with Moses and this action would cause them to trust Him always. God told him to have the people consecrate themselves two days. Have them wash their clothes, and to be ready on the third day. The Lord told Moses He would come down on Mount Sinai for all the people to see. He was to place boundaries for the people around the mountain and command them not to be inquisitive into the mount or touch any area that God had not specified. Whosoever touches the mount shall be put to death (beast and people). On the morning of the third day, there was a thick cloud, thunder and lighting, and the sound of a loud trumpet blast. This event caused all the people to tremble. Following this great scene, Moses then led them out of the camp to meet God at the foot of the mountain. For He is a consuming fire. Mount Sinai was covered with smoke because God came down in the form of fire. The mountain shook violently, and everyone could hear the sound of the trumpet that grew louder and louder. Then Moses spoke, and the voice of God answered him.

God has not always revealed himself with such power and demonstration to His people in a loud voice. Being in a state of prayer daily committing ourselves to him, confessing and repenting of known and unknown sins and the only time any should tremble is when working out our salvation with fear and trembling. If the reaction is terror upon hearing God's voice, the response instead should be do His will.

There is another scene in the Bible where God speaks audibly. Imagine being in a quiet pasture beside the still water of the Jordan River. Finding a group of people there listening to John the Baptist who preached saying, "Repent, for the kingdom of heaven has come near. This is he who was spoken of through the prophet Isaiah: A voice of one crying in the wilderness, 'Prepare the way for the LORD, make his path straight" (Matt. 3:2-3).

John was called the forerunner of Jesus by preparing the people to receive salvation. John was a simple man but probably thought to be different, because he was known to dress in camel's hair attire, a leather girdle and his diet were locusts and wild honey. He didn't mind being considered weird. John had sold out for Christ. He was in the world but not of the world. John the Baptist was going around the regions of Jerusalem, Judea, and Jordon, where people were asking for forgiveness of sins and being baptized by him. While he was out preparing the way, who shows up was spectators known as the Pharisees and Sadducees, who came to the baptism not to be Baptist but to get in the way. John immediately responded by saying:

> Oh generation of vipers, who hath warned you
> to flee from the wrath to come? Bring forth.
> Therefore, fruits meet for repentance:And
> think not to say within yourselves; We have
> Abraham to our father: for I say unto you, that
> God is able of these stones to raise up children
> unto Abraham. And now also the ax is laid
> unto the rootof the trees: therefore every tree

which bringeth not forth good fruit is hewn
down and cast into the fire. I indeed baptize
you with water unto repentance. But he that
cometh after me is mightier than I whose shoes
I am not worthy to bear: he shall baptize you
with the Holy Ghost, and with fire: Whose fan
is in his hand, and he will thoroughly purge his
floor, and gather his wheat into the garner, but
he will burn up the chaff with unquenchable
fire. (Matthew 3:7-12)

John the Baptist let them know he saw their trickery and their works dealing with his adversaries quickly. He knew that all that he would and could do was nothing compared to Jesus who was born to die for the sins of the world. God in due time was going to separate the righteous from the unrighteous. God chose and revealed his will to Apostle Paul when he commissioned him concerning the salvation of men by Jesus Christ. "And he said The God of our fathers hath chosen thee, that thou shouldest know his will, and see that Just One, and shouldest hear the voice of his mouth" (Acts 22:14).

He only knew the will of God as revealed in the law. However, did not understand the indwelling spirit, until that day. God's message was open to save sinners by faith in Jesus Christ. That was the message that Apostle Paul had to preach to the gentiles. This scripture shows that God spoke to Paul audible and directly on the road to Damascus. God's ways are more advanced than ours; Most cannot even understand the vast knowledge of him or why he loves such a sinful world. Moreover; that HE inhabits the prayer, praise, and worship of his people not because of our worthiness, but because HE is worthy of our praise.

Another way God reveals Himself is through a still, small voice. This particular day Elijah had just proved the power of the supreme God who was challenged in 1 Kings 18:20-40. Triumphantly, Elijah showed the people he served the greatest the Lord he is God. Elijah showed the power of prayer, praise, and worship to fight the enemy. Then he took the prophet of Baal and slew every one of them at the brook of Kishon, for they had sinned and caused that nation to sin. That day God had shown His hands as powerful through the Prophet Elijah even gave him supernatural strengthen to run thirteen miles further ahead of Ahab who was riding on a chariot. God will provide you with the strength and courage to make it past your situations. He answers Elijah in a sprint, running past his situation to the next challenge.

Meanwhile, the wicked queen Jezebel got wind of what happened from King Ahab that her prophets were dead at the hands of the prophet Elijah. She sent word by messengers to the prophet Elijah telling him; he was next to die. Elijah did what all fleshly humans would do, he begins to run for his life. He even prayed to die but by the hands of the Lord. How dare she think after all Elijah had been through she would get the spoil. On the way, he stopped and dropped off his servant in the city of Beersheba. He keeps moving a day's trip into the wilderness where he sat and slept under a broom tree. Quickly, while Elijah slept an angel touched him and said: "Arise and eat." Jehovah-Jireh had brought Elijah a cake and water, as He had in other times. After Elijah had eaten and laid down, the angel returned a second time and told him to eat again for strength for the journey ahead was too great for him. Elijah needed supernatural strength. For he was able to go forty days and forty nights without food. He then found a cave at Mt. Horeb for shelter for the night. Then the voice of the Lord spoke to him and asked, "What are you doing here, Elijah?"

Everywhere we go is not always where God wants us to be, but He still provides for His namesake. Elijah started talking to God about the works he had done for HIM. Elijah thought he alone was faithful. In his depression, he thought he was the only one faithful. Elijah thought that once killed there would be no one else. God told Elijah, "Go out and stand on the mountain before the Lord." Moreover, then the Lord passed by, and strong wind broke off some pieces of rock from the mountain, but the Lord was not in the wind. Then, after the wind, there came an earthquake, but the Lord was not in the earthquake. Following the earthquake, a fire, but the Lord was not in the fire but after the fire was a still small voice. Elijah became knowledgeable that God is not just the God of the spectacular. At times He only reveals His work in the sound of gentle stillness. Elijah did not realize that God was in the lives of many people working in them in many different methods. This effect by natural disaster changes represented the trials and tribulation in life, but God is faithful to see us through wholly and gently.

Jacob is alone in Haran. He has fled his home after deceiving his father and stilling Esau, his brother's birthright. Esau is aggressively in quest of killing him. Jacob lies down for the night, in the darkness, far from home, and places stones under his head for pillows to sleep and this is where the dream transpires. He dreams of a ladder set up from earth to heaven where God's angels were ascending and descending on the ladder. The Lord identifies Himself as the God of whom Abraham and Isaac both believed. God revealed to him that the land he slept on was Jacobs and that he would give to his offspring. His descendants, the nation of Israel would be like the dust of the earth and spread from the west, and the east to the north and the south. Most importantly he told him that, "I AM with you" right when he was running away from the penalties of his lie. God chose then to reiterate His promises. God favors even when we're undeserving of His mercies. "God is not a man, that he should lie; neither the son of man, that he should repent: hath he said, and shall he not do it? or hath he spoken, and shall he not make it good?" (Num. 23:19).

The ones who live in Christ can be encouraged by these words. God will not lie and will not renege on his promises to His people.

> "What shall we then say to these things? If God be for us, who can be against us? He that spared not his own Son, but delivered him up for us all, how shall he not with him also freely give us all things? Who shall lay anything to the charge of God's elect? It is God that justifieth. Who is he that condemneth? It is Christ that died, yea rather, that is risen again, who is even at the right hand of God, who also maketh intercession for us." (Romans 8:31-34)

God has done everything for us; all our adversaries are powerless. God gave the ultimate by giving His son, which proves He will freely give us all things. Christ fully justified us when He died on the cross as a ransom. No one can condemn or charge us because no one can separate us from His love.

The power of prayer, praise, and worship can be such a dynamic, humbling, and intricate action at the same time. It is so unique that every single one of us can pray our different way and still, our loving God hears everyone. "Blessed be God, which hath not turned away my prayer, nor his mercy from me" (Ps. 66:20).

God does not always reveal himself in significant ways. It is essential for us to get into the routine of noticing the smallest things during the day. When struggling to hear his manifestation, there is a need to take time during the day to get to a quiet place and request him to reveal himself in our life. Do not try to lean to our own understanding as the Bible tells us in Proverbs 3:5. Sometimes He

53

shows himself through messages that are preached by ministry and friends may provide the word of knowledge. Other times, He may speak directly to us. Walking down the path of life may seem challenging at times. God does not want us going down the wrong trail or feeling alone and on our own carrying everything by ourselves. It may take time for the Lord to reveal his answer but he will always answer providing clarity. "For God, who said, 'Light shall shine out of darkness,' is the One who has shone in our hearts to give the Light of the knowledge of the glory of God in the face of Christ" (2 Cor. 4:6).

God knows us and his plan for our lives is not in chaos, but he wants to bring us to His expected end. The Lord does not want us living in a state of worry and threat; he will always answer and help us find peace. Always shining His light in a dark world. "Then you will call upon Me and come and pray to me, and I will listen to you" (Jer. 29:12 NIV).

God will always search man's heart and reveal its true nature. God wants us to pray and repent to Him. Through the power of prayer, praise, and worship everyone must continue to seek God's will in their lives and wait for His spirit to reveal the promises. The test and trials of this life are the things that test the heart of man. It is not for God but for our making. However; it is a must to pay attention to the revelation of God speaking in the test and after the trial. Throughout the test, everyone must consult God for His will.

God sometimes uses dreams to communicate and reveal His strategy, to further His plan, and to put His people in places of influence. Joseph is one of the most renowned dreamers and one of the most famous dream interpreters in the Bible. First recorded dream as a young dreamer cited in Genesis 37:5-7. Joseph has a dream and tells his brothers. They already didn't like him because he was their father's favorite. This dream made them hate him the more. His dream tells them of a future event. The dream expresses that they all were in the field binding bundles of grain when Joseph bundles stood up vertical and his brother's bundles stood up encircling him in obeisance. Which signifies that one day that all his brothers would bow down to him. The scripture says the last shall be first and the first shall be last; read Matthew 20:16.

Answers to prayers sometimes reveal themselves in visions and dreams. Sometimes solutions to our questions through prayers are not even sought after, but a sovereign God reveals Himself anyway. "Oh, the depth of the riches and wisdom and knowledge of God. How unsearchable are his judgments and how inscrutable his ways" (Rom. 11:33).

The just shall live by faith in God because our wisdom does not match God's. It is beyond our comprehension of how the youngest child can rule the older.

Why, someone starting in church, that you may now teach later could become a bishop or an elder over you. Coming before him in humility because all matters to Him. Always seek God's plans for our lives. He told us in the last days His sons and daughter would prophesy some would see visions, some dreams. All this will involve much prayer, praise, and worship.

PRAYER AND
FASTING

When seeking God for answers and healing, the inability of impartations of the blessing fails, due to the decrease in faith. The book of Acts, chapter one verse eight, tells us that after the Holy Ghost comes upon us, we shall receive power. The power given was not for personal gain, but it is the power for Godly living. This power was given for a new task for believers to take the message of the gospel to the ends of the earth. Christ demanded his disciples to carry the word of the gospel no matter the circumstances to others. Our job is not to convince people but to tell them the truth of the good news. This power is given by the Holy Ghost that abides in the hearts of men that obtain the gift of the Holy Ghost by faith.

The lack of the application of faith that was given by the power of the Holy Ghost when prayer, praise and worship go forth, will allow the manifestation process of the spirit that produces blessing such as, lame to walk, the dumb to talk, financial benefits. The list goes on, and by faith take the limits off. The gift to perform miracles comes from God. The application and the increasing of our faith have to be taught by the Holy Ghost. Faith saves us. There are three components of saving faith one is having the understand to know our need for salvation and two that cognitive acceptance that our belief is true. Third, applying the things that faithfully identify with our lives. Totally, immersing ourselves in Gods will and trust what he says and use what He means to our survival.

When praying, all must immerse themselves in the will of God and trust that what's ask in faith is done. Every person has received a measure of faith when they accept the gift of the Holy Ghost. "For I say to every man that is among you, through the grace given unto me, not to think of himself more highly than he ought to think but to think soberly according as God hath dealt with every man the measure of faith" (Rom. 12:3).

Let us not be so prideful in what gifts or blessings God has bestowed on us so as lose sight of God's grace by faith. Our faith will grow, but stay in the Word to receive the further manifestation of God's power, is the lifeline. One should never get caught up in a prideful spirit and miss the mark of the high calling. God gives everyone the capability to believe that Jesus died on the cross for their sins and His death is the foundation of our Christian faith, after; receiving the gift of the Holy Ghost, Jesus continues to impart confidence supernaturally during times of crisis to get us through life's many challenges. When studying, meditating, praying, and fasting God will move mountains out of our lives.

Mark 9:22 speaks of a father young son was overtaken by a demonic spirit. This demonic spirit would throw this man son into the fire and the water regularly. The man begins to tell Jesus, how he had brought his son to His disciples, and they could not cast out

58

the evil spirit. Then Jesus responded and said, "O faithless and perverse generation. How long shall I be with you? Bring him hither to me (Mark 9:19). This faithless action rendered by the disciples provoked Jesus, yet Jesus's focused was still on the child's care. He expounded on the fact that despite his one-on-one teachings and healing in His disciple's presence they still lacked understanding of the application of faith. Through the Holy Ghost living inside of us, everyone can have a one-on-one experience of teaching and talking to Him in prayer. Jesus can lead us on His path of righteousness for His namesake. Much like Jesus's disciples, the same problem may exists today among people not understanding the knowledge of how faith works in prayer, praise, and worship.

After Jesus rebuked the demonic spirit, the healing took place and, the boy was no longer tormented by the demonic spirit. Then, Jesus's disciples came to Him and asked why they could not cast the demonic spirit out of the man's son. Jesus replied, "Because of your unbelief: for verily I say unto you, If ye have faith as a grain of mustard seed, ye shall say unto this mountain, Remove hence to yonder place, and it shall be remove, and nothing shall be impossible unto you" (Matt. 17:20).

The disciples could not purge the demon because of their lack of faith. Jesus said to His disciples that all they needed was faith the size of a mustard seed. This equates to a small amount of faith. Prayer, praise, and worship, and the Word of God will renew the mind and faith increased. "According to Romans10:17, faith comes by listening to and comprehending God's word." Those who did not receive the manifestation of God's grace heard the Word of God, the power of God was present but the disciples failed to appropriate it.

The mustard seed when it grows becomes the largest among plants. In contrast, our faith can start out small, but with continuous prayer and fasting, it can lead to our spiritual gifts growing to a surmountable potential according to God's will. Beginning to thank God for the small starts because they can become great if God is in it. "For we dare not make ourselves of the number, or compare ourselves with some that commend themselves: but they measuring themselves by themselves, and comparing themselves among themselves, are not wise" (2 Cor. 10:12).

We are incapable of knowing how to measure faith accurately without God. Man tries to measure himself by his own opinions as well as compares himself to others. God searches and knows man inward and outward.

The disciple's lack of faith was not because they did not cognitively understand what Christ stood for, but their lack of understanding was of the power of prayer. Furthermore, the lack of one's confidence in prayer is a sign that you are probably not praying enough. Self-reliance is more prevalent, opposed to relying on the everlasting God.

Jesus explained to the disciples the formula for casting out this kind of demonic spirit was through prayer and fasting. Now fasting sometimes refers to self-discipline and voluntary abstinence from food and drink for a period. Fasting humbles the flesh when its done to please the supreme God. Fasting and praying breaks the power of the flesh and demoniac spirits. Jesus was a man that fasted and prayed. The scripture tells us that Jesus was driven into the wilderness by the Holy Ghost to be tempted by the devil; read Matthew 4:1-10.

Before being tempted by the devil, Jesus fasted for forty days and night. Jesus as the son of man gave us an example in showing there is power in fasting and praying. Once Jesus had completed his forty days and night of prayer and fasting, God allowed the devil to show up to tempt Jesus. Just like the Holy Ghost directed Jesus to fast and pray the same Holy Ghost will communicate to us to fast. Fasting prepares us and guides our path through opposition coming to us to face. Many of Gods test comes to us quicker while fasting and praying; having a higher chance of passing the test. Fasting and praying help us see through God's eyes and hear his voice with more clarity. Jesus through fasting and praying was able to speak God's word to overcome Satan. When calling on the name of Jesus, He can enable us to believe and rely on the power of His presence. Jesus told us when we fast in Mathew 6:16 not "If you fast" meaning to obey His sometimes we will have to fast. In the New Testament,

Paul's words direct each person who wants to communicate with God to "pray continually" read 1 Thessalonians 5:17. He also tells us that God has a divine open-door policy and encourages us to "always rejoice" (vs.16) and to give thanks in all situations. God calls us to joy and thanksgiving, and terms of faith in God through Christ secured in continual prayer. Jesus wanted His disciples and us to know that every moment is a prayer zone. Christ is the only One who can indeed help us.

And to let the oppressed go free, and that ye break every yoke? Is it not to deal thy bread to the hungry, and that thou bring the poor that are cast out to thy house? When thou seest the naked, that thou cover him; and that thou hide not thyself from thine own flesh? Then shall thy light break forth as the morning, and thine health shall spring forth speedily: and thy righteousness shall go before thee; the glory of the LORD shall be thy reward. (Isaiah 58:6-8)

Fasting and praying when presented to God with good intent will loose, undo or set free the oppressed. It is worship still in taking care of the poor who are cast down and hungry. Fasting and praying should draw us closer to Gods will not self-will. During the time of the scripture, the people were not observing God in this manner. Verse eight says if we give more thought to our duties and responsibilities to the Kingdom of God, then a new day would come forth that our wounds or these light afflictions, are healed quickly, and that God's glory would overshadow us. He would be a rear defense that will alert us in a time of trouble. He will be our God and will be His people that when we call, He answers speedily. His people are supposed to be there for others in their time of need by fasting and praying. "But as for me, when they were sick, my clothing was sackcloth: I humbled my soul with fasting, and my prayer returned into mine own bosom" (Ps. 35:13).

God promotes the combination of prayer and fasting as a path of power. It is proven that fasting works in the scripture. There is a need to embrace a season of fasting not only from food but from any fleshly desires that may entrap us. Praying and fasting increase the Christian spiritual appetite for more faithful prayer, praise, and worship to our God.

WHY KEEP PRAYING, PRAISE AND WORSHIPING GOD WHEN YOU DON'T GET THE ANSWER YOU SEEK?

What happens when the results you seek when praying do not come to fruition? Why not? Second Samuel 11-12 chapter says King David decided when most Kings would go out to battle not to go at that time. The reason that Kings in the lands choose to go in battle during spring is that there was an assurance of good weather and an abundance of food along the journey. Instead, King David sent Joab and his army to besiege the Ammonite's capital city Rabbah without him. King David remained at Jerusalem pampering himself in the good life, while his soldiers were camping in open fields out to battle. An Idle mind is the devil's workshop. Many people have lost their lives, families, and friends for being in the wrong place at the wrong time. David gets up to take a stroll about the time he would have been sleeping had he been out on the battlefield. "For we hear that some among you walk in idleness, not busy at work, but busybodies" (Thess. 3:11 ESV). This kind of people never use their time wisely, but they like to stand in the way of others' progress.

Idleness births sin. David was strolling on the roof of his palace and saw something that brought pleasure to him and aroused all his senses. David saw a young woman bathing on her roof. The

64

scripture, which rarely describes physical appearance says that the woman was gorgeous. David being arrogant uses his authority to inquire, *Who is this woman?* He did not ask whose wife is she because that did not make a difference. Pride comes before destruction; read Proverbs 16:18. The servant came back with an answer and told him her name was Bathsheba, wife of Uriah the Hittite.

This was a time when David should reflect on God's Word and acknowledge God's will and asking for direction which would have enabled him to not sin. David was facing adultery. However, there is always a door open to avoid sin. That door is prayer and fasting. "Men should always pray and not faint" (Luke 18:1). David overrode the truth in his arrogant state and thought his status as the king said he could disregard sin. He sends for Uriah's wife and commits adultery with her. For David had thought it would be a one night of pleasure and he would be a rolling stone. There are always consequences to sin. "His iniquities will capture the wicked, And he will be held with the cords of his sin" (Prov. 5:22).

Every sin is a transgression to God, and he cannot allow sin to come in the presence of holiness. David's sin displeased God, and there will be no rest for the sinner. Bathsheba became pregnant and sent word to David. David came up with a plan to kill a dedicated soldier that seems like a good idea to the wicked. He sent for Uriah for a cover-up. However, Uriah was more righteous than King David for he refused to go home to sleep with his wife and live-in pleasure. Since his fellow contemporaries were out risking their lives for them in battle, he knew that on the battlefield was where he belonged.

It is essential as a soldier in the Army of the Lord to understanding our footing in God. Girding our side handles with truth and our feet planted on the gospel of truth. However, David continues to try and break Uriah by giving him too much to drink. King David's effort failed to trick Uriah into sleeping with Bathsheba his wife to cover up King David's fornication. Bathsheba was pregnant – but not by her husband.

"Thou shalt not covet thy neighbor's house, thou shalt not covet thy neighbor's wife, nor his manservant, nor his maidservant, nor his ox, nor his ass, nor anything that is thy neighbor's" (Exod. 20:17). Now, David resorts to a set-up that has Uriah killed in battle. David told Joab the commander of the army, to put Uriah in the heat of the fight. Not only did he ask him to place him on the front-line David even wanted him to leave him alone without back up. Once Uriah was deceased David married Bathsheba to make it appear that the child was legitimate. He Continues to cover up the adulterous scandal. However, for Uriah, it was an honor to die on the battlefield for the Lord.

"Nothing in all creation is hidden from God's sight. Everything is uncovered and laid bare before the eyes of him to whom we must give account" (Heb. 4:13 NIV). All are under complete exposure and defenseless before God. Each one must give an account to an omnipotent, omnipresence, and omniscience of God. Although David managed to hide his sin before the people, God knew all about it. David was going to have to give an account of his crime.

Then the Lord sent Prophet Nathan to David to tell him of his sins that God sees and knows. Nathan knew that David as the king had the highest judgment and court of appeal for the people. So he uses that knowledge against David to bring him to God's truth. Nathan told David a story of ethics about one rich and one poor man. Nathan knew that this type of story would appeal to David's intellectual appetite. Nathan said there was a wealthy man and a poor man who lived in the same town. The rich man owned many sheep and cattle. The poor had nothing more than one little lamb that he bought and raised. The lamb ate and drank from a poor man table and even slept with him. The lamb to the poor man became a household pet in another word; he was family. "A righteous man regardeth the life of his beast: but the tender mercies of the wicked [are] cruel" (Prov. 12:10). A godly man would not put even an animal to needless pain, our life matters to God. For God so loved the world that He gave His Son and then His Son gave His life. A human's life is more significant than animals, every one of us all should love one another as God loves His sheep.

The Prophet Nathan visited King David, and while there he began to dazzle the King with him acting as if He needed wisdom from the King. When in a King's presence all must make him feel great and unique. The prophet tells what seems to be a hypothetical tale about a traveler the goes to a rich man for food, and the rich man refused to take from his herd or flock to prepare a meal for the traveler. Instead, he took the poor man's lamb and made it for the man that came to him. Nathan told the story in such a way that reminiscent of chapter 11: 4 when King David had sent messengers, then took Bathsheba. Upon hearing this story, David became very angry with the rich man in the story. He said to Nathan the man that done this evil shall surely die. The rich man execution would have happened under normal circumstances. David was deserving to die for the sins of adultery and murder. "And the man that commits adultery with another man's wife, even he that commits adultery with his neighbor's wife, ...shall surely be put to death" (Lev. 20:10).

Here, David was the guilty one, not Bathsheba; he took her from her home. He also set up Uriah's sudden death. He might as well draw his sword and killed Uriah himself because blood was still on his hands. "For this, thou shalt not commit adultery, Thou shalt not kill, Thou shalt not steal, Thou shalt not bear false witness, Thou shalt not covet; and if there be any other the commandment, it is briefly comprehended in this saying, namely, Thou shalt love thy neighbor as thyself" (Rom. 13:9).

God's commandments clearly state what sins were punishable by death. David had broken the sixth, the seventh, and the tenth commandments that cover adultery, murder, and covetousness.

Nathan then told David that he was that man. Nathan had tremendous courage to speak these words because David just had a man killed. David was upset; he could have reacted to Nathan and had him killed. The Prophet Nathan continued to talk to David. Nathan told him that God anointed Him as King of Israel and kept Saul from killing David. God gave King David a house, wives to live peacefully in Israel, that should have been enough. If that was not enough all King David had to do was ask, and God said he would have given him more. Sometimes it's essential to take a step back to see if our convictions have been compromised. David was a great man of God yet was overcome by selfish ambitions. A need to check ourselves to see if the leading is God or by self-proclaimed agendas. "For behold, the LORD is about to come out from His place to punish the inhabitants of the earth for their iniquity; And the earth will reveal her bloodshed and will no longer cover her slain" (Isa. 26:21).

Prophet Nathan replied that God said since David had taken the Lord's commandment lightly. Despite everything, the King of Israel had to bow to God's discipline. Every knee shall bow to the justice of our Lord. Because of sin, David would receive three judgments for his sin. God's judgment was as followed; bloodshed would never leave his house while David lived. David's family would bring adversity against him. Next, David's wives would be taken by another. "For nothing is secret, that shall not be made manifest; neither anything hid, that shall not be known and come abroad" (Luke 8:17).

David's iniquities were isolated, but God's punishment and correction were public. The word of God is the gauging stick God always uses for judgment. Instantly, David asked forgiveness for his revealed sins. That is one of the reasons the Bible witness that David was a man after God's own heart and why David wrote Psalms 51:

> Have mercy upon me, O God, according to thy
> lovingkindness: According to unto the multitude of
> thy tender mercies blot out my transgressions. Wash me
> thoroughly from mine iniquity, and cleanse me from
> my sin. For I acknowledge my transgressions: and my sin.
> *is* ever before me. Against thee, thee only, have I sinned,
> and done *this* evil in thy sight: that thou mightiest be
> justified when thou speakest *and* be clear when thou
> judgest. Behold, I was shapen in iniquity; and in sin did
> my mother conceive me. Behold, thou desirest truth in the
> inward parts: and in the hidden part thou shalt make me to
> know wisdom. Purge me with hyssop, and I shall be clean:
> wash me, and I shall be whiter than snow. (Psalm 51:1-7)

This scripture depicts David's response to Nathan's rebuke. A petition for God's mercy concerning the situation of David's confession. Compassion is the appropriate request for a confessing sinner. In this Psalm, David laid out his guilt before God and cried out for God's forgiveness. David committed not to repeat this same sin. David could rest or sleep because the sin was always before him. All these words: transgression, iniquity, and sins let us know that this was a severe offense against God.

David was deserving of the death penalty for murder and adultery. David received God's divine forgiveness for his sins, but he still had to live with the consequences. "Be not deceived; God is not mocked: for whatsoever a man soweth, that shall he also reap" (Gal. 6:7)." If the Lord ignored David's sins without consequences, then unbelievers would say that God was unholy because he let Christians do anything.

After the Prophet Nathan departed David's house. The child born of his adulterous relationship with Bathsheba was struck with illness. The child must not have been alive long because he never received a proper name. David is beginning to plead with the Lord for the child. David fasted and prayed all night laying on the floor before God. The elders of his house tried to get him to eat but he would not.

The child died on the seventh day. David had a longing for the child to live because he knew that would be proof of divine favor by God restoring David. God did not answer David's prayer by allowing the child to live because of his prayers and fasting. David had sinned, and this was one of the consequences of those sins. Once David realized the child was deceased, he picked himself up out of his sorrow and begin to humble himself and begin to worship the almighty God. He made his way to Mount Moriah to worship.

> This is an evil among all things that are done under the sun
> that there is one event unto all: yea, also the heart of
> the sons of men is full of evil, and madness is in their
> heart while they live, and after that, they go to the dead.
> For to him that is joined to all the living there is hope: For
> a living dog is better than a dead lion. For the living know
> that they shall die: but the dead know not anything neither
> have they any more a reward; for the memory of them is
> forgotten. (Ecclesiastes 9:3-5)

Where there is life, there's hope so prayers should continue undiminished. There should not be any thought to stop praying until an answer is received. God could intervene at the last moment. God's judgment is righteous and because His righteousness, everyone should praise Him even when they do not obtain the results they seek. There was a judgment on David, so God did not answer his prayers by healing the child. The consequences of David's sin were that his first son by Bathsheba died. However, when the child was dead, David humbled himself under the mighty hands of God and became satisfied with God's grace without continuing in pain.

Samson had a lust for women and shook himself seeking the presence of the Lord, but God was not there. King Saul had a passion for power and money and found that seeking other Gods lost him his Kingdom and the presence of the Lord upon him. The spirit of the

Lord will not dwell on any unclean things. God expects all who sin to realize they have sinned and repent. "'There is no peace,' says my God, 'for the wicked'"(Isa. 57:21).

When losing family members, a close friend there is an emptiness that can be replaced by the love of God, sure it hurts but God's compassion when embrace fails not. That is the reason a must for pray, praise, and worship in releasing our difficulties to Jesus.

CONCLUSION

In conclusion, God's design has always been to lead us to a deeper understanding that in His timing will result in a life of greater rewards on earth; an eternity of rewards in the kingdom to come. God is calling with urgency for men to kneel, yielding to prayer, praise, and worship.

> All scripture is given by inspiration of God and is profitable for doctrine, for reproof, for correction and for instruction in righteousness: 17. That the man of God may be perfect, thoroughly furnished unto all good works. (2 Timothy 3:15-17)

God provides the scripture to promote righteousness and to motivate us to control carnality natures to His will. God's instruction given lacking nothing Apostle Paul was instructing Timothy in this passage teaching how to be able to go through test and trial with success. The scripture will correct or restore, turn around and heal in mind and spirit which trains us to live in righteousness. We must not waiver or be double-minded in our prayers. If we lack the knowledge, we need to ask God to reveal his word to us which is his laws; read James 1:5. The power of prayer rests in praying in accordance to God's will. God's will be that man should pray and not faint. God's word says that "Ye have not because ye ask not" (James 4:2). The power in prayer results is not in wishes granted on earth. Prayer is bonding with the will of God while praying. God will not fulfill his will until prayer happens. The prayer request is made in the land while God's voice answer from heaven perspective. We should pray from earth to heaven because this world is not our home. The power of prayer is not forcing our petition against God's will. Again, prayer is dialoguing the will of God channeling it from our mouth. Prayer does not modify what God has already predestined it only achieves what God has ordained. Now, if we do not pray it will change results because we did not petition because God mandated that we ask anything in his name in prayer.

The power of prayer is the strength that gives us freedom of action, the right to act; the use of Jesus's name is unrestricted and is absolute through our prayer praise and worship. What makes prayers powerful is giving petitions to the rule of Jesus Christ. Praying in His name is more than just saying it as loose jargon.

When praying, use His name we take on his identity, He is righteousness, and He is power and authority, because no one can come to the Father but by Him. See when we send a powerful, passionate prayer up to God, it gets results because God sees we recognize the authority he has given us in prayer; read James 5:16. Prayer is conversation or action that pursues to activate a relationship with the true God of worship, and we should pray without ceasing; read 1 Thessalonians 5:17. "But ye shall receive power, after that the Holy Ghost is come upon you: and ye shall be witnesses unto me both in Jerusalem and in all Judea, and in Samaria, and unto the uttermost part of the earth" (Acts 1:8).

This power and the authority are released to us as a gift once we receive the Holy Ghost, empowering us to take the good news to the ends of the earth that others might be saved, through the blood of Jesus Christ. Prayer can be either individual or communal and take place in public or in private. According to Psalms Notes from Tabernacle Bible Institutes, "Prayer may be oral or mental, ejaculatory or formal" and may involve the use of words, song or complete silence. As we grow in our love for Jesus Christ, we will naturally desire to talk to Him more. Prayer language may take the form of a hymn, or a spontaneous utterance in the person praying. Prayer is a privilege and the means of promised blessings.

Prayer should be made to deter evil of all kinds; pray on behalf of others request; pray giving thanks to all he has done. We should pray for those who have rule and dominion over us that world peace may be conserved and well pleasing in the sight of the Lord. It is God's desire that all have a long life richly because of the knowledge of his truth. Prayer is something that God admonished us to do unceasingly, with the mechanical inclination that should never be abandon for any reason. Praying without ceasing is knowing that God is present always. Prayer helps turn hearts to God. In that, it changes perspective. God joins hearts to him. He gives us grace and assistance in time of need, changes attitudes and the universe surrounding us. Prayer should be a pretty normal activity that should be just like talking. Speaking to the Lord is prayer, but prayer is more than just saying what we feel. Prayer is for the strong, the low, the rich, and the poor. Prayer can also be a way to ask God for this or for that. God tells us that He gives us what we ask for, within his will. Genuine prayer is communication with God, the importance is that thoughts be in agreement between His and ours. Asking in faith according to his will; read John 14:13-14.

Prayer should be directed only to God and prayer should pull us to God. There is power in his name. Making a commitment to Christ, through the strength of the Holy Spirit changes the heart and from a changed heart comes a new yearning for what is wanted and needed. Living according to the flesh comes naturally because we are born with a sinful nature and shaped with immoralities; read Psalm 51:5.

> "O wretched man that I am! Who will deliver me
> from this body of death? [25] I thank God—through
> Jesus Christ our Lord! So then, with the mind, I
> myself serve the law of God, but with the flesh the
> law of sin" (Rom. 7:24).

We were unfit to live and unfit to die until Christ came to save, oh wretched man. Once Christ died for us. Oh, but the blood of Jesus, thank God for the blood! The saving power of the blood, without the blood there is no remission of sins. If asked, Jesus forgives sin. If we repent, He will remit our sins, and we can receive his redemption power by receiving the gift of the Holy Ghost. Jesus teaches us how to walk and talk in the Spirit and not to satisfy the desires of the flesh; read Acts 2:38.

In Matthew 6:9-15, Jesus' teaches "The Model Prayer" this brief prayer shows how to seek the sovereignty of God from a heaven perspective on earth. This prayer challenges us to lay aside the personal quest for gain because for us is that God's will, not our will, be done. Just as Jesus gave up his fleshly desires and submitted to the will of the Father, likewise follow His example and surrender; read Luke 22:42. Prayer should happen daily to acknowledge God's authority. Basic needs from the Lord can be meted when asked, learning it is only through the Lord that, we are God's progeny. He is our Creator; we must worship him; read Acts 17:28.

Pray not to be seen, but should be a personal visitation with God. Where there is no prayer, there is no grace. God will give unmerited favor openly. He does not give everything asked, only because he knows we do not need it, and it is not good for us; read Matthew 6:6. Pray in secret, and receive a blessing openly that all will see. Making a commitment to the Lord, confessing and repenting of sins of commission and omission because we should work our soul deliverance with fear and tremble (Phil. 2:12). The essence of God is known and taught by praying; the more prayer happens it will tap into his power. "For I determined not to know anything among you, save Jesus Christ, and him crucified" (1 Cor. 2:2).

Digging deep is knowing Him and Him knowing us because "out of the belly will flow rivers of living water" (John 7:38). Meaningful prayer causes sustainment of spiritual life flowing from the natural man to the spirit-filled man. Instead of losing a life, but gaining "life more abundantly" (John 10:10). That is why when praying, it should be in the name of Jesus because in the name of Jesus Satan trembles; read James 2:19.

Jesus put on mortality that we might put on holiness, to become the sons of God. Something about when hearing the name of Jesus that sends waves of regenerate energy of thoughts that might have never been considered. The revelation of one receives by knowing Him by the name of Jesus reveals the uniqueness of God through Christ too many. "They saw no man, save Jesus only" (Matt. 17:8).

Jesus is the only mediator, Savior, and Redeemer, the only Prophet, Priest, and King. Who can only save and will dwell with his people when no one else can?

Secondly, praise must be a part of prayer because it signifies that we trust God. Even if he does not answer what we ask, we understand that we are called for, His purpose and His plans for the kingdom. We understand while praying if we praise it throws the enemy off its task. The devil cannot believe after going throw a trial still having joy. When taking burdens to the Lord and leave them there, believe. That relationship gets results because those willing come to him casting all cares of life upon the Lord.

Thirdly, praying, worshiping says submission to God's will. Worship covers every deed while praising God. Worshiping is true answers flowing from the heart after receiving an amazing revelation from God. Worshiping God in the Spirit and his truth because he is King of King and Lord of lords, His love is never failing. Prayer should start with praising and worshiping. Why because of He is holy, righteous all deserving. God is the God that heals, delivers, provides and regenerates.

Fourth, Kingdom praying is God s reining in our heart when we pray, to direct us. The kingdom of God is in the midst; read Luke 17:21. Where the King is, that is where His rule is recognized. When we pray, we must accept His will, express by letting his kingdom come and his will happen over our life.

The call to worship is not just individually but can also be communal honoring God in everything. When coming together to worship our purpose is to be a light to the nation, worshiping God at all times as an example. God's rule is what the kingdom means and not a place where he rules. There is an old saying that goes, *a family that prays together stays together.*

The day Jesus took Peter, James, and John, his brother, and led them up to a high mountain, they say Moses and Elijah and Peter thought that the kingdom had come. However, Jesus was establishing a new rule ending ancient evils making a fresh start. Through Jesus the kingdom God has arrived. So, when we pray,

80

praying in Jesus's name is paramount. Men and women were made to live in communion with God. *Kingdom praying* is prayer asking God to meet the needs of his people in Israel, America, and worldwide.

Fifth, forgiveness and confession must become an immediate functionality. This action must be decided before it happens. Not waiting for someone to ask for forgiveness. Humbleness of the heart has to be a matter of fact. Those that live by the code of a humble heart will not wear on emotional sleeves. The trigger for not asking is pride and anger. Forgiveness and confession display love for our fellowman. Confession is good for the soul. When we forgive, and confess God is placed on assignment. God promised that he would pay wages good or bad. "Vengeance is mine; I will repay, saith the Lord" (Rom. 12:19).

Confessing our sins shows our openness to an enormous God. Next, to petition God is to trust him by sharing issues in life through prayer. There is no certain way to petition God, but it should be the main task of the day to follow. Jesus model prayer begins by acknowledging "Our Father" giving honor to him and seeking first the kingdom of God. When petitioning God, it is the work of the Holy Ghost to plead with God for us in groans that cannot be said but directed. Petition God that He sends His protection, mercy, and truth to places persecuted, for righteousness' sake. Petition God for the hungry, diseased, rumors of wars and wars that God send His peace that surpasses all understanding. Petition God that we may forever be obedient and that the truth is not sent forth to compromise and submit to a spirit of deception. Our petition or supplications must implore God for something and should be with a passionate fervor that's hanging fuel for pray. Strictly speaking, a petition is not another form of prayer but an attitude that accompanies prayer.

Finally, prayer of faith, prayer of agreement and prayer of dedication or consecration, praise and worship, forgiveness, confession, there is much overlap in all these prayers. All should be a regular part of our talking to God. All are an inclusive act that involves prayer, praise, and worship honoring God. Prayer and praise are powerful because God is powerful. In that, He is God almighty, omnipotent, omnipresence and he can respond to what we ask in faith. To do what He thinks is right. Prayer was and is God's idea. God will never contradict His will because of prayer. The Creator is not obligated to respond to the creature's prayers that would violate his nature. The fear of God is the beginning of wisdom; read Proverbs 9:10. That is knowing in prayer that God does what is right to him and we must honor his will with prayer, praise, and worship.

God gave authority to release God's power through prayer. If we want God to move on Earth, we must ask because God has given authority; read Luke 11:9. To forbid or permit things on earth through heaven's gates through prayer; read Matthew 18:18. Our prayers are ushered up to glory to Jesus, Jesus paid it all; read John 14:6.

God made man in his image, just a little lower than the angels. Men were created to rule over God's creation on earth. However, through Jesus Christ man is restored that is those who trust in him. So, prayer transmits higher authority than any bosses' decision because God can move upon the hearts of men in answer to prayer. Through prayer, we can place all things under our feet and if we want God to move in are behave, just pray because it changes circumstances. The Apostle Paul prayer life often mentions throughout his epistles demonstrating he was either asking for prayer or praying for someone. "For God is my witness, whom I serve with my spirit in the gospel of his Son that without ceasing I make mention of you always in my prayers" (Rom. 1:9).

Alternately, he was asking for prayer "Brethren pray for us" (1 Thess. 5:25). He advocated prayer. Pray continuously; read 1 Thessalonians 5:17. He wanted everyone to know, understand the power of prayer that solidifies a relationship with the Lord through staying in continual counsel with Him through prayer.

Prayer is praise and worship. With this in mind, consider every Chapter as the framework of recommended steps to take, alone or with others, to build skills in becoming a power-filled continual prayer, praise, and worshiper of JESUS CHRIST. Please take a moment and dive into the word of God to absorb "The Power of Pray, Praise and Worship" in every situation.

Prayer, praise and worship must be for a purposeful cause. In developing the habit of on-purpose expressing to God all cares. When praying to God, it is a secret between Him and us. Prayer takes energy that must be shared with the Almighty God, no matter our location or our emotional and physical status. No matter the situation, our responsibility and pleasure are to use the power of prayer, praise, and worship. It is exciting to know every time when praying God is present with us. "For in him dwelleth all the fulness of the Godhead bodily. And ye are complete in him, which is the head of all principality and power" (Col. 2:9-10).

Learning to identify with Christ in such a way that because He is our friend naturally living by His will. Becoming more aware of the days ahead through God's voice in prayer. "Not as though I had already attained, either were already perfect: but I follow after, if that I may apprehend that for which also I am apprehended of Christ Jesus" (Phil. 3:12).

Making note that prayer changes more than things but people as well. Through prayer, our thoughts and ways are altered to do His will. Prayer is essential just as the air breathe is to the lungs and as oxygenated blood is to our heart. There are no restrictions in communications to God, who invites us to call upon His name whether coming, or going, or sitting still.

Prayer, praise, and worship are not about the human elements provided (clapping, shouting, preaching, etc.) and what is gained, but true worship is all about serving the Lord. Prayer, praise, and worship are about giving to God and getting His blessing.

Many have heard people say or maybe even used the phrase us in saying, "I did not get anything out of the service today." That is because they did not come to serve God because it's God who receives the worship. With our whole heart arise giving our all to Him. In our prayer, praise and worship let us acclaim the crucified Christ. True worship ascribes to the Lord what he deserves power, riches wisdom, strength, honor, glory, and blessing. In our prayer, praise and worship let us tell the Lord; that He is indeed worthy of all the praises. He never tires to hear these words from our lips. When worshiping using music it extols His death and music then leads us to the throne room of God, praise, prayer, and worship is our continuous activity.

> So, Joshua fought the Amalekites as Moses had ordered,
> and Moses, Aaron, and Hur went to the top of the hill.
> As long as Moses held up his hands, the Israelites
> were winning, but whenever he lowered his hands,
> the Amalekites were winning. When Moses' hands
> grew tired, they took a stone and put it under him
> and he sat on it. Aaron and Hur held his hands
> up-one on one side, one on the other so that his
> hands remained steady till sunset. (Exodus 17:10-12)

This next epic story in the Bible is another pinnacle of what prayer, praise, and worship express in total. It reveals in the battle to pray, praise and worship because God is on the throne, and in this battle, it draws on who God is and why prayer, praise, and worship are mandated by Him.

Israel engaged in battle with the Amalek. God prepares his people to be able to withstand their foe for the good of His kingdom. The Israelites had become weary in their journey and had stopped obeying God's commandments and feared not God they were in total rebellion. God has a way of getting his beloved attention. Rebellion is as the sin of witchcraft; read 1 Samuel 15:23.

A perfect invitation to Satan's lair, then and now. He has not changed his tactics. The Israelites had traveled through the desert of Sin and camped in a place called Rephidim. The word Rephidim means hands became weak and the people ask the question in verse seven "Is the Lord among us or not?" Israel lacked the power of faith that is why they were weak. Little did they know while they were complaining, Moses was praying (He knew I AM). Moses fasted and prayed to say, "O Lord, who will in the future spread Thy Law if Amalek succeeds in destroying this nation?

Moreover, with uplifted arms, (praise) holding the staff and pointing up toward heaven (worship). Rephidim was a place that the power of prayer prevailed amongst the rise and fall of a battle; read Exodus 17-8-16. Moses, the intercessor on the mount, came to experience that the weaponless hand of prayer was more powerful than armies. As one fight went on below with the ground forces, another combat went on the hilltop. Holding fast to God no matter how blistering the storm appears. We must be like an eagle in a storm, the scripture says, "But they that wait upon the Lord shall renew their strength; they shall mount up with wings as eagles; they shall run, and not be weary, and they shall walk, And not faint" (Isa. 40:31).

See, the eagle gets excited (he goes into praise and worship in anticipation of a storm. He begins to spread his wings, to wait, to wait, and to wait for it to come. Most birds are hiding in the trees but not the eagle. The eagle is in the air as the storm approaches the eagle spreads his wings. The storm grabs the eagle and takes him higher above the storm. The tempest is passing under him, and he is soaring above it. That is why the eagle is thrilled when a storm is coming because he knows it is going to take him higher. That is why the scripture says that if we wait on the Lord, he will renew our strength and will soar like an eagle in a storm. There is a blessing in the storm it will take us higher above our situation(s). Hardships make us strong.

Finally, in our praying, praising, and worshiping to Our God. Always communicating love and compassion for one another by interceding for them in prayer. Praying in faith, from our heart, often the needs for ourselves and others. Pray in specifics. Even though God knows everything; but He wants us to come to the throne of grace boldly, continuously. He likes to hear from us to understand our needs close and personal. He is a jealous God. He cannot stand for us to tell our neighbor before He knows our situations, troubles desires, and wants. He does not wish to have second-hand news. There should be such a need to be so close that the anticipation of waiting to tell him the good and the bad hurts us not to share it with Him immediately. Remember praying is talking to God. Having strong godly love for one another as the scripture says, "Love one another, even as I have loved you" (John 13:34).

An unselfish act on our part taking on the heart of God's character because "God is love." Zealously praying can and will change the situation in family, friends, and even hater's lives. There should be a time set aside to turn our plate down (fast) when circumstances are very severe or knocking at your home court, you may need to fast and pray, praise and worship. Not waiting for the battle to end but praying and praising Him in advance. Fasting will give, provide the antidote to go the distance to see the final results for the situation. If the results are wrong, fasting can provide the strength needed to take it and make it and shout hallelujahs because fasting energizes the spirit. If things are good or bad, our spirits can have hallelujah praises. To name a few Hallelujah Praises, Abraham interceded for the people of Sodom for the sake of his nephew Lot; read Genesis 18:23-33.

The Apostle Peter prayed for Dorcas, who was dead. She had a reputation for helping the needs of the people, and her untimely death was a tremendous loss. The Apostle Peter was summoned. He prayed, God heard, and her life was restored; read Acts 9:36-41. The people laid her in an upper chamber instead of burying her; they understood the power of prayer, praise, and worship. They put Dorcas in an upper room as a declaration to their faith they begin to cry and praise thinking on the things that she had made as things that were lovely and praiseworthy unto God for allowing them to meet such a woman of God.

There is life maintenance in reading the word of God because the bible is the only book that can actively make a change in lives. It is in God's Word that provides historical lessons, archeological and scientific discoveries, and facts about life can be found. The Bible is God's voice with His love. When picking up His Word and reading it, readers can hear His voice. It teaches us to pray, praise and worship from God's perspective when prayer is added with a sense of sincerity something will change.

When praying and reading God's word, readers can gain strength. Even when aching all over, the challenges facing loved ones, and fear that the situation won't change, temptation to believe that things won't change and that God won't respond. Our perception is understanding never underestimate the power of prayer, for our God who loves us will hear every cry, praise, and worship.

Prayer takes morals, discipline for the mind, emotions, and our self-will. The prayer of praise or adoration is a prayer giving honor and glory to God for the great I AM. Prayer, praise and worship must become a life style not a random effect. Not questioning His answers and just submit to Him in obedience. All of us must become convinced of God's Plan for our life that forgetting all our personal rights in favor of God's will becomes the daily norm. Genuinely praising the Lord requires us to focus on God's character while forsaking what all dread, what is mistaken in our lives, and the self-reliance. "Praise the Lord, for His mercy endures forever" (2 Chron. 20:15).

The Israelites were ready to give up, but they prayed and gained strength to seek directions from God when facing their attacker. While preparing for battle, King Jehoshaphat organized a choir to march out in advance of their enemy's army. The choir sang, "Praise the Lord, for His mercy endures forever." When the music started, Israel's enemies became confused and destroyed each other. Whether encounter a battle or feeling trapped, all can glorify our God in our hearts.

Most may not know how God will respond to our petitions but knowing that our Father longs for us to embrace His love and to trust in His faithfulness. Stay connected with the King through prayer, praise, and worship. By this conclusion, May God open up spiritual eyes and imparts a new level of understanding of the Power of Prayer, Praise, and Worship.

GLOSSARY

Anthropomorphism - Referring to God by human characteristic, the attribution of human traits, emotions, or intentions to non-human entities; the purpose of inanimate objects, animals, plants, or other natural phenomena or God.

Broom Tree - is, in reality, a desert shrub of the pea family.

Christians – Follower of Jesus Christ. (Acts 11:26; 26:28)

Confession- Openly admit personal wrongdoing. Confess to God and each other. Declare or acknowledge Jesu as Lord.

Consecrate- Devote, separate, set aside for worship or service to God. A person or thing consecrated. May also refer to the installation of a priest and offerings. (2 Chron. 29:31)

Despising the word of the Lord- to think light of, this is a sin that is done, as it were, done while looking God in the eye and shaking one's fist at Him.

Dreams- To have ideas or images in mind, in the state of sleep; with of before a noun; as, to the vision of a battle; to dream of an absent friend. Thought or experience while sleep. God can communicate with His people through dreams. (1 Kings 3:5)

Faith -Belief, trust (Mark 11:22). Faith in Jesus is essential for salvation. (Eph. 2:8-10)

Fasting- Fasting, sometimes done as a group or by individuals. Sometimes it was done for spiritual purposes, such as in connection with religious observance.

Flesh- something that is entirely human, limited to only a physical body and the physical strength it contains.

Forgiveness- Pardon or excuse a wrong. Cancel a debt. Give up a claim for revenge or resentment. Reestablish a broken relationship. To forgive is to trust others as if the wrong is forgotten.

Gleaning- Hebrew Law allowed the poor and strangers to gather grain or grapes left from a harvest. (Ruth 2:2)

God's Audible voice - heavenly or divine voice which proclaims Gods will or judgment. (Deut. 4:12)

Good News- Christ's death, burial, and resurrection bring salvation to all who respond in faith.

.

Gospel – Good news, Christian message about the life and sacrificial death of Jesus Christ that brings salvation to all who believe.

Handwriting on the wall - A phrase recalling an Old Testament story about Daniel. While a king was holding the Jews captive in the foreign land of Babylon, in the sixth century B.C., a mysterious hand appeared, writing on the wall of the king's palace.

Holy Ghost – God's Spirit. Lives within all Christians to help them, communicate God's truth to them, convict them of sin, convince them that God's ways are right, and comfort them when they are sad (John 15:26; 16;7-8, 13-15). God sent the Holy Ghost to guide us after Jesus left earth.

Humility – Freedom from pride. A humble person has the right view of God, self, and others. Humility is not weakness, but a strong quality praised in the Bible and commanded for all Christians. Humility shows trust in God.

Jealous– Intolerant of the rivalry of unfaithfulness; zealous or ardent. God declared Himself to be a jealous God demanding the faithfulness of His people.

Jehovah-Jireh – Jehovah will see or provide, Abraham gave the name to the place on which he had been commanded to offer Isaac, to commemorate the interposition of the angel of Jehovah, who appeared to prevent the sacrifice, (Gen. 22:14) and provided another victim.

Jesus- Savior, Jesus is the divine Son of God. He is eternal; that means He always was, is and will be. He is God pre-incarnated.

Justified – declared righteous and therefore innocent of all charges against us.

Kingdom is where God considered being a place where God's reign is complete. Refers to a king's authority or rule over a territory or the hearts of people.

Mist - (*n.*) Visible watery vapor suspended in the atmosphere, at or near the surface of the earth; fog, 2. (*n.*) Coarse, watery vapor, floating or falling invisible particles, approaching the form of rain as, Scotch mist.

Mustard Seed – An annual plant that grew quite fast and was popularly thought to have been the smallest of all seeds. However, positive identification cannot be made of the plant Jesus referred to in His parable of the mustard seed (Matt. 13:31-32). Christ used the parable to illustrate something that starts small and multiplies such as the kingdom of God. The mustard seed is not the smallest seed known today, but it was the smallest used by farmers and gardeners in the Holy Land at that time. Under favorable conditions, the mature plant could reach about ten feet (three m) in height. Using the mustard see as a metaphor for the kingdom no doubt shocked Jesus' audience, who expected God's kingdom to be tremendous and expansive. The idea seems to be that the small beginning of the church will eventually culminate in ignificant growth. The parable accordingly foreshadows the growth of the church into a world power. The mustard seed is one of the tiniest seeds found in the Middle East, so the conclusion is that the amount of faith needed to do great things is very small indeed. Just as in the parable of the mustard seed (Matt. 13:31–32), Jesus uses rhetorical hyperbole to make the point that little is much when it comes from God. The Lord signifies that a very slight real faith, which he compares to the mustard seed, that smallest of grains, would be of power sufficient to accomplish what seemed to them impossible. In other words, he says, "If you have any real faith at all, you will be able to win the victory over yourselves necessary for a perpetual loving judgment of others."

Nazarite law – The Nazirite was one who made a special vow to the Lord for a time of unusual devotion to God. There were three vow prohibitions: Total abstinence from all substances from the grapevine (wine) 2. No, cutting the hair 3. No contact with the dead no matter who died. (Num. 6:2-8)

Obeisance - Prostrate (especially reflexive, in homage to royalty or God) -- bow (self) down, crouch, fall down (flat), humbly beseech, do (make) obeisance, do reverence.

Omnipotence - all-powerfulness · almightiness · supremacy · preeminence · supreme power · absolute/unlimited power · undisputed sway · divine right.

Omnipresence - present everywhere at the same time: the omnipresent God.

Omniscience - the state of knowing everything.

Panoplia - The word represents the ancient Greek πανοπλία. The phrase πᾶν means "all," and ὅπλον, "arms." Thus "panoply" refers to the full armor of a hoplite or heavy-armed soldier, i.e., the shield, breastplate, helmet, and greaves, together with the sword and lance.

People of God – to believe in him; all Christian are a chosen generation; sanctified by his spirit. He sent his son Jesus to die on the cross as a ransom.

Perseverance- Keeping on, not giving up, lasting consistency, endurance. (Eph. 6:18) The implication of steadfastness, patience, persistence is confirmed by the use of the verb proskartereo, to attend consistently, continue unswervingly, adhere firmly, and hold fast to. In its spiritual application it always has to do with continuance in the Christian way, particularly in relation to prayer (Acts 1:14, Rom. 12:12)

Petition – Aitema, from aiteo, to ask is rendered "petitions" prayer

Power- Hebrew-dynamic- Strength, authority. God revealed His power through history, acts of nature, individual lives, and the Holy Spirit. Jesus revealed God's power through His miracles and forgiveness.

Praise – hala (Hebrew) (strong 1984), thanks; boast; Praise of God is the acknowledging of His perfections, works, and benefits. Praise and thanksgiving are generally considered as synonymous, yet some distinguish them thus: praise properly terminates in God, on account of his natural excellences and perfections, and is that act of devotion by which we confess and admire His several attributes; but Thanksgiving is a more contracted duty and imports only a grateful sense and acknowledgment of past mercies. We praise God for all His glorious acts of every kind, that regard either us or other men; but we thank Him, properly speaking, for the instances of His goodness alone, and for such only of these as we are in some way concerned.

Proseuchomai – the Greek word for prayer, to pray to God, i.e., Supplicate, worship, make a Prayer is a converse with God; communion with God. Prayer may be oral or mental, ejaculatory or formal. It is a "beseeching the Lord" (Exod. 32:11); "pouring out the soul before the Lord" (1 Sam. 1:15); "praying and crying to heaven" (2 Chron. 32:20); "seeking unto God and making supplication" (Job 8:5); "drawing near to God" (Ps. 73:28); bowing the knees" (Eph. 3:1).

Righteousness - Righteousness is the state of moral perfection required by God to enter heaven. However, the Bible clearly states that human beings cannot achieve righteousness through their own efforts: "Therefore no one will be declared righteous in God's sight by the works of the law; rather, through the law we become conscious of our sin." God the Father is righteous (just); Jesus Christ his Son is the Righteous (Just) One; the Father through the Son and in the Spirit gives the gift of righteousness (justice) to repentant sinners for salvation; such believing sinners are declared righteous (just) by the Father through the Son, are made righteous (just) by the Holy Spirit working in them, and will be wholly righteous (just). The Old Testament says that God is righteous. In Psalm 7:11a we read "God is a righteous judge." The word righteous in the Hebrew is "tsaddiy" which means just, lawful, and correct. The word righteous in the New Testament comes from the Greek word "dikaios" which means observing divine laws or upright, faultless, innocent, and guiltless. These are all descriptive of God Himself and no human has any of these attributes inherent in themselves even though we can do things that are upright and observe the divine laws like the Ten Commandments while not being able to obey them all.

Saints - Holy ones set apart. All true Christians are saints. Not perfect people but those who have accepted Jesus as Lord and Savior.

Sanctification- God's cleansing process to make a person whole and like Jesus. It affects both character and conduct. Part of God's will and plan.

Sanctified jargons- To use scriptures and prayer like slogans so the appearance is like a Christian (a pretender) an external seeming that does not rightly represent the heart on the inside.

Self-righteous – considered one's religious practices to be better than another religious practice.

Sin- missing the mark of God's will by choice and because of human weakness. Action or attitude that disobeys God betrays Him or fails to do well. Sin brings the pain.

Sozo - (4982) Saved, to save, to deliver, keep safe, and sound, to rescue from anger or destruction, delivered from the judgment of sin (Ps.18:3). Regeneration and salvation.

Still small voice – Inner voice, people think of the still little voice, they imagine hearing verbal instructions. Voice of God or other heavenly agents offering human beings' suggestions for understanding and action.

Tactic- an action or strategy carefully planned to achieve a specific end. Strategy · scheme · stratagem · plan · set of tactics · maneuver · course/line of action · method · program · expedient · gambit · move.

Theophany's – Is a visible manifestation of God, and we usually think of it as temporary.

Vision – a special message or revelation from God. An image could contain instructions or interpretations or present-day or future occurrences. (Dan. 2:19)

Vow concerning a woman who is married- If a woman enters into a vow to the law after marriage, the husband could overrule the vow. His silence would allow it to remain in force.

Wicked Woman – Daughter of Belial or without value and this term is also used as a proper name for Satan (see 2 Cor. 6:15). Sinful, evil, wicked, worthless, wrong, cruel, malignant.

Worship- Shachah, Adore, obey, reverence, focus positive attention. Enjoy the presence of God. Any action or attitude that expresses praise, love, and appreciation for God. Worship can be expressed through obedience (prayer, praise, and worship) and the way we treat people. Worship can be private or public. Two ways to worship is prayer and praise.

SOURCES

Bernard, D. (1956). *The Oneness of God* (ed., Vol., pp. 27-28). Hazelwood, Mo: Thomas Nelson Inc.

Bernard, D. (1987). *The Message of Romans* (ed., Vol., pp. 20-21). Hazelwood, Mo: Thomas Nelson Inc.

Dockrey, Karen, Godwin Johnnie and Godwin, Phyllis. (2007). *The Student Bible Dictionary* (ed., Vol., pp. 1-251). Uhrichsville, OH: Holman Bible.

Lane, P. (2013). *Psalms Notes* (ed., Vol., pp. 4). Huber Heights, Ohio: Tabernacle Bible Institute.

Thompson, F. (2007). *The Thompson Chain-Reference Bible* (5th Improved ed., Vol., pp. 1-1910). Indianapolis, IN: B.B. Kirkbride Bible Co., Inc.

Unger, Merrill and White, William. (1970). The Nelson's Expository Dictionary of the Old Testament. Nashville, TN: Thomas Nelson, Inc.

Unless otherwise noted all Scripture references in this book are taken from the King James Version of the Holy Bible

Zodhiates, S. (1994). *Hebrew-Greek Key Word Study Bible* (Second Revised ed., Vol., pp. 1590-2284). Chattanooga, TN: AMG International, Inc.

SCRIPTURE

1. I acknowledged my sin unto thee, and my iniquity has I hid. I said, I will confess my transgressions unto the Lord; and thou forgavest the iniquity of my sin (Ps. 32:5).

2. Blessed is he whose transgression is forgiven, whose sin is covered. Blessed is the man unto whom the Lord imputeth not iniquity, and in whose spirit, there is no guile" (Ps. 32:1-2).

3. (To the chief Musician upon Jonathelemrechokim, Michtam of David, when the Philistines took him in Gath.) Be merciful unto me, O God: for man would swallow me up; he fighting daily oppresseth me. 2 Mine enemies would daily swallow [me] up: for [they be] many that fight against me O thou most High. 3 What time I am afraid, I will trust in thee.4 In God I will praise his word, in God I have put my trust; I will not fear what flesh can do unto me. 5 Every day they wrest my words: all their thoughts [are] against me for evil. 6 They gather themselves together, they hide themselves, they mark my steps, when they wait for my soul. 7 Shall they escape by iniquity? in [thine] anger cast down the people, O God. 8 Thou tellest my wanderings: put thou my tears into thy bottle: [are they] not in thy book? 9 When I cry [unto thee], then shall mine enemies turn back: this I know; for God [is] for me. 10 In God will I praise [his] word: in the LORD will I praise [his] word. 11 In God have I put my trust: I will not be afraid what man can do

unto me. 12 Thy vows [are] upon me, O God: I will render praises unto thee. 13 For thou hast delivered my soul from death: [wilt] not [thou deliver] my feet from falling, that I may walk before God in the light of the living? Psalm 56:1-13

4.   Oh come, let us worship and bow down; let us kneel before the Lord, our maker (Ps. 95:6).

5.   However, thou, when thou prayest, enter into thy closet, and when thou hast shut thy door, pray to thy Father which is in secret and thy Father which seeth in secret shall reward thee openly (Matt. 6:6).

6.   And when he was demanded of the Pharisees when the kingdom of God should come, he answered them and said, the kingdom of God cometh not with observation: Neither shall they say, Lo here! Or, lo there! For, behold, the Kingdom of God is within you (Luke 17: 21-22).

7.   Father, if thou will be willing, remove this cup from me: nevertheless,not my will, but thine, be done (Luke 22:42).

8.   And whatever you ask in My name, that I will do, that the Father may be glorified in the son. If you ask anything in My name I, will do it (John 14:13-14).

9.   But I see another law in my members, warring against the law of my mind, and bringing me into captivity to the law of sin which is in my members (Rom. 7:23).

10.   Therefore, I exhort first of all those supplications, prayers, intercessions, and giving of thanks be made for all men, 2. For kings and all who are in authority, that we may lead a quiet ad peaceable life in all godliness and reverence. 3. For this is good and acceptable in the sight God our Savior, 4. Who desires all men to be saved and to come to the Knowledge of the truth. 1 Timothy 2:1-4

11.   If any of you lack wisdom, let him ask of God, that giveth to all men liberally, and upbraideth not; and it shall be given him (James 1:5).

12.   The effectual fervent prayer of a righteous man availeth much (James 5:16).

13.   For the accuser of our brethren is cast down, which accused them before our God Day and night (Rev. 12).